SQE 1 PREP COURSE

BUSINESS LAW AND PRACTICE

BY ANASTASIA & ANDREW VIALICHKA

First Edition

Published by MetExam
https://metexam.co.uk

ISBN: 978-1-917053-07-5

ISBN: 978-1-917053-26-6 (Hardcover Book)

The information provided in this book is subject to change without notice and should not be construed as a commitment by the authors or the publisher. While every effort has been made to ensure the accuracy of the information contained herein, the authors and publisher assume no responsibility for any errors or omissions, or for damages resulting from the use of the information contained in this book.

This publication is designed exclusively for educational purposes, serving as a comprehensive study aid for individuals preparing for the SQE 1 examination. It should not be construed as offering legal advice or as an authoritative resource on legal matters. Its primary objective is to facilitate learning and exam preparation.

Authors: Vialichka, Anastasia; Vialichka, Andrew
Title: Business Law and Practice. SQE 1 Prep Course / Anastasia Vialichka, Andrew Vialichka
Description: First Edition | London: MetExam, 2024
Identifiers: ISBN 978-1-917053-07-5
Subjects: LCSH Business Law and Practice—United Kingdom—Examinations, questions, etc. | Business Law and Practice—England—Examinations, questions, etc. | Business Law and Practice—Wales—Examinations, questions, etc. | Common Law in Business Practice—United Kingdom—Case Studies. | Legal education in Business Law and Practice—United Kingdom. | Legal education in Business Law and Practice—England. | Legal education in Business Law and Practice—Wales.

INTRODUCTION

INTRODUCTION

Welcome to the foundational stone of your journey towards becoming a solicitor in England and Wales. This text is meticulously crafted as part of a comprehensive MetExam training course designed to prepare you for the Solicitors Qualifying Examination. It lays out the intricate legal tapestry you are about to navigate, providing you with the essential knowledge and analytical tools needed to succeed.

Embrace the learning that awaits, and let this book be your guide and ally on the path to legal proficiency and excellence.

Throughout this text, authors draw upon a wealth of legal scholarship and case law. While specific contributions are not cited in the body of the book, a comprehensive list of all works referenced can be found at the end. These references serves as an acknowledgment of the significant works that have informed this text and as a resource for readers seeking to explore the subject matter further.

CHAPTER 1. ESSENTIAL FACTORS IN SELECTING BUSINESS ENTITIES

1. Limited Liability Company & LLP

A key advantage of forming a Limited Liability Company or a Limited Liability Partnership (LLP) compared to a sole proprietorship or a traditional partnership is the aspect of limited liability extended to its shareholders.

When a company is incorporated, it becomes a separate legal entity, accountable for its debts, an arrangement often referred to as the 'veil of incorporation'. Shareholders' financial exposure is limited to the amount they have invested in shares. In situations of company insolvency, shareholders with fully paid-up shares are not required to contribute additionally to the company's financial liabilities.

However, there are instances where this protective veil can be lifted, holding shareholders or directors personally responsible for the company's debts. This concept will be further explored in subsequent sections.

In contrast, sole proprietors and general partners lack limited liability protection. They bear personal responsibility for all business-related debts, which could endanger their assets and business investments. This responsibility is collective and individual in partnerships, permitting creditors to demand full debt repayment from any or all partners involved.

Imagine a company, 'BrightTech Ltd', where investors have purchased shares. If BrightTech Ltd incurs significant debts or faces legal action, the shareholders' liability is limited to the value of their shares.

For instance, if a shareholder invested £10,000 in BrightTech Ltd, that is the maximum they could lose. In contrast, if a sole trader, like Jane, who runs a bakery, faces debt, her assets, like her home, could be at risk to cover the business debts.

2. Registration and Compliance

The privilege of limited liability is accompanied by the necessity for more stringent regulatory and filing requirements. Companies and LLPs must register with Companies House and fulfil various filing responsibilities, including submitting annual financial statements and confirmation statements.

These obligations often result in extra costs and may require hiring a company secretary for administrative support and accountants and auditors for financial documentation and review.

By contrast, sole traders and general partnerships are not bound by these rigorous filing requirements, facilitating a more rapid and cost-efficient business establishment process. They also have the advantage of not being required to disclose their financial statements publicly, providing a measure of privacy for their business operations.

'GreenScape LLP', a landscaping business, must register with Companies House and adhere to strict filing protocols, such as submitting annual financial reports. This necessitates additional administrative support and potentially hiring a company secretary.

On the other hand, a sole trader like Tom, a freelance graphic designer, does not need to follow such stringent filing processes, enabling him to set up his business more swiftly and with less bureaucratic overhead.

3. Taxation Overview for Different Business Entities

The taxation of sole traders and partnership members is conducted through income tax, with their entire taxable income subject to applicable tax rates.

In contrast, companies are subject to corporation tax, and their shareholders are taxed on dividends. Regarding taxation, LLPs are more similar to partnerships, with members being taxed on income rather than the LLP being liable for corporation tax, as with companies.

'Crafty Creations', a partnership of artisans, pays income tax on their profits, with each partner filing tax returns individually. In contrast, 'Innovate Inc.', a tech company, pays corporation tax on its earnings, and its shareholders pay income tax on any dividends they receive.

4. Securing Finance through Borrowing

Companies and LLPs generally find it more straightforward to access financing, as they are often perceived as more financially stable by lending institutions.

This is partly due to their ability to provide floating charges on their assets, security not available to sole traders and general partnerships. A floating charge encompasses present and prospective business assets, offering lenders greater security than a fixed charge on static assets.

'BuildIt Construction LLP' can secure a loan by offering a floating charge on its assets, like equipment and accounts receivable. This is more appealing to banks than a sole proprietor like Emma, a florist, who cannot offer such comprehensive security, making it harder for her to obtain large business loans.

5. Managing the Business

There is no distinction between ownership and management in sole proprietorships and general partnerships. However, companies have a clear separation between owners' (shareholders) and managers' (directors) roles. It is common for an individual to hold both positions, especially in smaller or family-run businesses.

Managing a Partnership:

The Partnership Act of 1890 sets out the partnership management framework, detailing partners' responsibilities and liabilities. Partners, however, have substantial freedom to manage the business as per their agreement, allowing for considerable operational flexibility.

'The Design Duo', a partnership between two architects, operates based on a partnership agreement they drafted, outlining each partner's role and responsibilities, demonstrating the flexibility in partnership management.

Corporate Governance in Companies:

Under the Companies Act 2006, specific directorial requirements exist for private (minimum one director) and public companies (minimum two directors). Directors are subject to extensive legal duties and must comply with the company's articles of association, which act as the company's internal rulebook.

These articles, which can be tailored to suit the company's needs, usually include guidelines on the conduct of board meetings, the appointment of directors, and their removal.

'Quantum Computing Ltd.' is a private company with one director, Sarah, who complies with the company's articles of association. These articles specify how board meetings are conducted, what director responsibilities are, and how directors are appointed or removed.

CHAPTER 2. OVERVIEW OF GENERAL PARTNERSHIPS

1. Establishing a General Partnership

A general partnership is an option exclusively for two or more entities in business structures. According to the Partnership Act 1890, a partnership is a relationship among individuals or entities engaged in a joint business venture to generate profit.

This definition encapsulates **three essential criteria for a valid partnership:**

(a)   The involvement of **at least two parties**;

(b)   The **collaborative operation** of a business;

(c)   **The mutual objective** of realising a profit.

Emily and John decide to start a catering business together. Emily has experience in culinary arts, and John has expertise in event management. They agree to combine their skills and resources to provide event catering services. Their collaboration fulfils the three criteria for a general partnership: Emily and John are involved, they are operating the catering business together, and they have the mutual goal of making a profit from their services.

1.1 Participants in the Partnership

In the context of a partnership, the term' persons' extends beyond just individual humans to include corporate entities like companies.

Therefore, a partnership can be established between individual people or between an individual and a corporate entity when they engage jointly in a business endeavour.

A small tech startup, Tech Innovations Ltd., and an experienced software developer, Alex, decided to collaborate on developing a new mobile application. Tech Innovations Ltd. provides the necessary capital and technical resources, while Alex brings in his software development and design expertise.

This partnership between a corporate entity (Tech Innovations Ltd.) and an individual (Alex) to jointly develop a product for profit illustrates how 'persons' in the context of a partnership can include both individuals and corporate entities.

1.2 Joint Business Operations

The' business in common' concept integrates two distinct notions: 'business' and 'in common'. Here, 'business' refers to commercial activities such as buying and selling goods or offering services in return for payment. This can range from managing a clothing store to running a law firm.

The 'in common' element emphasises the collaborative nature of these activities. It implies that all parties involved in the business work together, sharing the right to make decisions, partake in profits, and manage other business aspects collectively.

Consider two friends, Alice and Bob, who decide to open a café. Alice has expertise in baking, while Bob is skilled in coffee making and customer service. They agree to share responsibilities: Alice manages the bakery section, and Bob handles the coffee and service area.

They make joint decisions on menu items, pricing, and business hours. Their operation of the café, sharing decision-making and profits, exemplifies 'business in common'.

1.3 Purpose of Profit Generation

Central to forming a partnership is the shared objective of generating profit. A partnership is not considered valid if profit-making is not one of its primary goals.

Notably, the intention to achieve profit is crucial; the actual success or failure of the business in making a profit does not affect its status as a partnership.

Additionally, it's worth noting that the parties involved do not need a specific intention to form a partnership. The critical requirement is their joint intention to engage in a business venture to make a profit.

Sarah and Raj established a graphic design firm. Their primary goal is to provide design services to clients and earn revenue. Even though the firm did not make a profit in its first year due to high startup costs and competitive pricing, its intention was always to generate profit.

Despite the initial lack of actual profit, this intention to profit qualifies their venture as a partnership under the legal definition.

1.4 Absence of Formal Requirements

It's important to highlight that forming a partnership doesn't mandate a written agreement, even though many partnerships choose to establish one.

Additionally, as mentioned earlier, submitting any documentation to Companies House is unnecessary. A partnership is set and can commence business operations as soon as the three criteria are met.

Let's consider two friends, Mia and Zoe, who decide to start a handmade jewellery business together. They begin by pooling their resources, agreeing on roles, and selling their creations online.

Despite needing a written partnership agreement or registering their venture with Companies House, Mia and Zoe have effectively formed a partnership as soon as they meet the three criteria: they are two persons carrying on a business in common with the intention of making a profit.

Their business is legally recognised as a partnership from the moment they start their operations, demonstrating that a formal agreement or registration is not a prerequisite for establishing a partnership.

1.5 Indicative Evidence of Partnership through Profit Sharing

Determining the existence of a partnership can sometimes be ambiguous. In such situations, the courts examine the specific circumstances to assess whether there was an intention to conduct a business jointly. According to the Partnership Act, receiving a share of a business's profits is typically considered prima facie evidence (initial proof) of a partnership.

However, this **presumption is not applicable in some instances:**

(a)   If the profit share is a repayment of a debt,

(b)   If the profit share is compensation for an employee or agent (for example, if a sandwich shop owner agrees to give the shop's manager a 10% profit share, this does not inherently make the manager a partner);

(c)   If the profit share is an annuity paid to a deceased partner's survivor or someone who has sold the business's goodwill.

Agreement on Loss Sharing

It's important to note that while an agreement to share losses may indicate an intention to establish a partnership, it is not conclusive evidence.

Moreover, there needs to be an agreement regarding loss sharing to preclude the formation of a partnership. Consider, for example, Arthur and Gwen, who started a used board game shop. They should have discussed how they would handle potential losses, perhaps due to their confidence in their venture. Despite this omission, they still effectively created a partnership.

1.6 Situations That Do Not Constitute a Partnership

The Partnership Act clarifies that simply co-owning property with one or more individuals does not automatically result in a partnership, regardless of any agreement to share profits from that property.

Additionally, more than sharing gross returns alone is required to establish a partnership.

1.7 No Mandatory Contribution

While it is common for partners to invest capital or assets into a partnership, it is not mandatory for someone to become a partner. Contributions, though typical, are not a prerequisite for partnership formation.

Unlimited Partnership Size:

Legally, there is no upper limit on the number of individuals or entities participating as partners. This allows for partnerships to include any number of partners without restriction.

2. Absence of Distinct Legal Identity

Contrary to entities like companies or LLPs, a partnership lacks an independent legal personality separate from its partners.

As a result, partners in a partnership are subject to unlimited personal liability for the debts and obligations incurred by the partnership.

3. Power to Obligate the Partnership

The Partnership Act encompasses numerous provisions addressing the dynamics among partners and the management of the partnership.

Notably, most of these rules serve as default guidelines and are applicable only if the partners haven't established their agreements to the contrary. This means that partners have the flexibility to modify or enhance the terms set out in the Partnership Act through a bespoke partnership agreement, although they are not compelled to create such an agreement. The following discussion primarily concentrates on the default provisions as outlined in the Act.

3.1 The Role of Partners in Legally Binding the Partnership

Within the framework of a partnership, the business activities are managed by the partners. This aspect is critical for legal academics, including those preparing for qualifications like the SQE and in practical legal applications.

It's vital to understand under what circumstances a partner's conduct can legally commit the firm in terms of contracts or tort law. The Partnership Act draws upon Agency law principles and provides the regulatory basis for these scenarios. It delineates that every partner is an agent for the partnership and their fellow partners.

Under Agency law, an agent's ability to bind the principal (the partnership, in this context) depends on whether they possess authorised power, which can be categorised as either actual or apparent.

(a) **Actual Authority.** According to the Partnership Act, a partnership is legally bound by actions that:

- Are executed with the explicit intention of obligating the firm,

- Are carried out by an individual whom the firm has expressly authorised to perform that Act.

In many cases, partnerships operate under agreements that assign specific powers and responsibilities to certain partners, effectively bestowing them with actual authority.

This authority can also be established through a collective decision by the partners, authorising a particular partner to perform specific tasks. Furthermore, the courts acknowledge the concept of implied actual authority, which comes into play when partners habitually perform certain activities without formal authorisation but with the tacit consent or acquiescence of the other partners.

(b) **Apparent or Ostensible Authority.** Under the Partnership Act, the actions of a partner that align with the typical business activities of the firm are legally binding on both the firm and the other partners.

Exceptions to this rule occur in **two scenarios:**

• When the partner in question lacks actual authority for the action they undertook,

• When the third party involved is either aware that the partner lacked such authority or did not recognise or believe that the individual was a partner of the firm.

Determining whether a partner's action falls within the usual business activities involves an objective analysis: would a reasonable third party view the action as standard for a business of this type and expect a partner in such a firm to have the authority to undertake such an action?

(c) **Sole Liability of a Partner for Unauthorised Actions.** Should a partner enter into a contract with a third party without the necessary authority, the partner alone incurs personal liability, not the partnership. This liability is attributed to a breach of the warranty of authority, a principle established in agency law. When a partner purports to act on behalf of the partnership in a contractual context, they implicitly guarantee to the third party that they are authorised to do so. If it is subsequently revealed that the partner lacked such authority, they become personally accountable for this misrepresentation.

3.2 Responsibility for Debts and Misconduct

Partners are subject to unlimited personal liability for the partnership's debts in cases where the partnership itself lacks the means to settle its debts using its assets. This collective liability enables creditors to seek repayment of the entire debt from any one partner or all partners collectively.

Similarly, partners are accountable for tortious acts. If a partner, while conducting standard business operations or with the authorisation of the other partners, commits a tort, both the partnership and the partners are equally liable. In such scenarios, the liability of the partners is both joint (as a collective) and several (individually).

Imagine a scenario involving a partnership, "City Gardening Services," consisting of three partners: Anna, Ben, and Carla.

The partnership faces financial difficulties and accumulates a significant debt to a supplier, "Green Thumb Supplies," amounting to £50,000. Unfortunately, "City Gardening Services" does not have sufficient assets to cover this debt.

In this situation, "Green Thumb Supplies" has the legal right to recover the debt from all partners. They could choose to pursue Anna, Ben, Carla, or a combination of them for the entire amount of £50,000. This exemplifies the joint liability aspect, where any partner can be held responsible for the whole debt.

Additionally, while working on a project, Ben negligently damages a client's property, resulting in a tort claim against the partnership. Since Ben acted in the course of the partnership's business, not only is the partnership liable for his actions, but Anna and Carla also share this liability. This is an instance of joint and several liability, where each partner is individually and collectively responsible for the wrongdoing.

Therefore, the injured party can claim the total amount of damages from any of the partners or the partnership as a whole.

3.3 Responsibilities of Joining and Departing Partners

(a) **Joining Partners.** According to the Partnership Act, a partner joining an existing partnership is not held liable for the partnership's debts or obligations incurred before joining. However, it's important to note that the new and existing partners can mutually agree to terms that differ from this statutory provision through a contractual agreement.

It's also crucial to recognise that the induction of a new partner into a partnership requires the unanimous consent of all current partners.

Additionally, the ability of partners to expel a fellow partner from the partnership is not inherent. This power must be explicitly granted, usually outlined in the partnership agreement, to be enforceable.

Imagine a partnership, "Brighton Bookstore," run by two partners, Lucy and Omar. They decided to expand the business and bring in a new partner, Raj, to contribute additional capital and expertise.

Joining Partner (Raj):

When Raj joins "Brighton Bookstore," he is not automatically liable for debts or obligations that the bookstore had incurred before his joining. For instance, if the bookstore had a debt of £10,000 to a supplier accrued before Raj became a partner, he would not be responsible for this debt unless he and the existing partners, Lucy and Omar, agree otherwise in a contractual agreement.

Lucy and Omar must also agree to Raj's induction into the partnership. Without the consent of either Lucy or Omar, Raj cannot become a partner.

Suppose the partners encounter disagreements after a year, and Lucy and Omar wish to expel Raj from the partnership. Unless their partnership agreement explicitly grants them the power to remove a partner, they cannot legally force Raj out of the partnership. If such a clause exists in their agreement, they can proceed with the expulsion as per the agreed terms.

(b) **Outgoing Partners – Debts Incurred Before Leaving.** When a partner departs from a partnership that continues its operations, the outgoing or retiring partner remains accountable for any debts or obligations the firm incurred prior to departure.

While the departing partner and the remaining firm may reach an agreement absolving the former from these obligations (such as through a release or a 'hold harmless agreement' where the firm agrees to indemnify the retiring partner), this agreement does not impact the retiring partner's direct liability to third parties. A 'novation' agreement involving the third party's consent is required for third-party liabilities to be waived.

Emma is a partner in a consultancy firm, "Eagle Consulting." She decides to retire and leave the partnership, which continues to operate with the remaining partners. At the time of Emma's departure, the firm had a debt of £20,000 to a software vendor. Even after her retirement, Emma remains liable for this debt, as it was incurred while she was a partner.

However, Emma and the remaining "Eagle Consulting" partners agree that the firm will indemnify her for this liability. While this agreement protects Emma from claims by "Eagle Consulting," she remains liable to the software vendor unless they agree to a novation, releasing her from the obligation.

(c) **Outgoing Partners – Debts Incurred After Departure.** When a third party interacts with a firm after a change in its membership, they are entitled to consider all seemingly involved partners as still part of the firm until they are notified of the change. Therefore, to avoid liability for future debts of the firm, a retiring partner must actively announce their retirement. Direct notice should be given to existing creditors, while public notice, typically through an advertisement in the London Gazette, is necessary for potential new customers.

Suppose a partner retires without being known to a third party who has dealings with the partnership. In that case, that retiring partner is not liable for debts the partnership incurs with that third party after their retirement date.

John was a partner at "Green Gardens," a landscaping company. He retired, and the company continued its operations. John ensures that his retirement is announced in the London Gazette and informs all existing creditors of his departure. Six months later, "Green Gardens" incurred a debt with a new supplier who was unaware of John's retirement. Since John has given proper retirement notice, he is not liable for this new debt.

However, if John hadn't given the appropriate notice, he could potentially be held responsible by the new supplier, who might have assumed John was still a partner when the debt was incurred.

4. Representation of Partnership Involvement

This principle addresses situations where an individual who is not an actual partner represents themselves as such or allows others to believe they are a partner in a firm.

In these cases, they can be held liable as a true partner to any third party who extends credit to the partnership based on this misrepresentation. This liability arises from financial transactions and broader interactions, such as the supply of goods, based on the trust placed in the person's misrepresented partnership status.

Moreover, the 'holding out' concept can also apply to partners who have retired but have not effectively communicated their departure to current and prospective clients. This situation can occur if they fail to remove their name from the firm's notices, website, or official stationery, leading others to believe they are still active partners.

In such instances, they may still be held liable for transactions made by the firm under the assumption of their ongoing partnership.

Claire, who is not a partner at "Tech Innovations," a software development firm, tells clients she is a business partner. One client, believing Claire is a partner, enters into a sizeable contract with "Tech Innovations" based on Claire's supposed authority and reputation.

Later, when issues arise with the contract, the client discovers that Claire is not a partner. However, Claire can be held liable for any obligations to the client under the contract, as she misrepresented herself as a partner, and the client relied on this representation in making the deal.

5. Ownership and Treatment of Partnership Property

Establishing a partnership often involves the partners contributing resources to facilitate the commencement of business activities. While financial contributions are expected, partners may also supply tangible assets like equipment or premises.

It's crucial to distinguish whether such assets are owned by the partnership collectively or remain the personal property of individual partners, as this distinction significantly impacts how these assets are handled upon the dissolution of the partnership.

Assets owned personally by a partner will naturally revert to that partner upon the dissolution of the partnership.

Conversely, any assets a partner provides that become integral to the partnership's operations are considered partnership property. These contributions are viewed as capital investments into the collaboration and are recorded in capital accounts maintained for each partner. These accounts reflect each partner's share of contributions, profits, and losses within the partnership.

5.1 Legal Definition Under the Partnership Act

The Partnership Act defines partnership property as assets either initially contributed to the partnership or subsequently acquired for its operations and within the scope of its business activities.

Without a differing agreement, any property purchased with the partnership's funds is considered partnership property. Similarly, property registered in the partnership's name is deemed to be owned by the partnership.

Imagine a graphic design firm, "Creative Designs," formed by two partners, Alice and Bob. Alice invests £10,000, and Bob contributes high-end design software and computer equipment. Later, they used the firm's funds to purchase a new printer and lease office space in "Creative Designs."

The £10,000 cash contribution by Alice, Bob's software and equipment, the new printer, and the leased office space are all considered partnership property as per the Partnership Act. These are original contributions or assets acquired for and during the partnership's business.

5.2 Role of Partners' Intent

It is insufficient to assume that property used in the partnership's business automatically becomes partnership property. The transition of property, brought into the partnership, into partnership property or its retention as the personal property of an individual partner hinges on the intentions of the involved parties.

For instance, if a partner brings personal property into the partnership at its inception, it will only be regarded as partnership property if there is an explicit or implied agreement among the partners.

Bob, before forming "Creative Designs," owned a high-quality printer. He brings it into the office for business use, but there is no explicit agreement between Alice and Bob about the ownership of this printer. Even though it's used in the partnership's business, it remains Bob's personal property, as there was no expressed or implied agreement to make it partnership property.

In contrast, if Alice and Bob had agreed verbally or in writing that the printer Bob brought in would be part of the firm's assets, it would then be considered partnership property. This decision would be based on their mutual intention regarding the printer.

5.3 Exclusive Use for Partnership Object-
ives

The assets designated as partnership property must be utilised and managed by the partners solely for the objectives and operations of the partnership. This usage must align with the stipulations and intentions set out in the partnership agreement. The partners are obligated to ensure that these assets are not employed for personal gain or purposes outside the scope of the partnership's business.

Consider a partnership, "Cityscape Architects," formed by two architects, Mia and Noah. They decided to lease a high-tech architectural software program and a downtown office space as part of their partnership agreement. The software and office space are paid for from the partnership's funds and are thus considered partnership property.

Mia and Noah must use the architectural software and the office space exclusively for the projects and operations of "Cityscape Architects." For instance, they use the software to design buildings for their clients and office space for meetings, design work, and other business-related activities.

However, if Mia starts using the software for freelance projects unrelated to "Cityscape Architects," or if Noah uses the office space for a side business or personal activities, they would be violating the principle that partnership property must be used only for partnership purposes. This misuse could lead to disputes or legal complications within the partnership, mainly if such actions affect the partnership's profitability or reputation.

5.4 Protection of Partnership Property from Individual Partner's Debts

When it comes to the individual debts of a partner unrelated to the partnership, creditors of that partner cannot claim or execute against the partnership's assets. In other words, partnership property is shielded from being used to settle a partner's liabilities.

However, these creditors can petition a court for an order to charge the indebted partner's interest in the partnership. Should such an order be issued, the creditor is entitled to receive any profit distributions that would typically go to the indebted partner.

However, this does not grant the creditor any status as a partner. Consequently, the creditor does not gain any rights to participate in the management of the partnership.

Additionally, a partner cannot bequeath partnership property through a will, as the partnership, not individual partners, collectively owns this property.

Let's consider "Gourmet Catering," a partnership run by two chefs, Lisa and Mark. Lisa has incurred a significant personal debt outside of the collaboration due to some unrelated investments. Her creditors, seeking repayment, discover her interest in "Gourmet Catering."

The creditors realise they cannot directly seize assets like the partnership's kitchen equipment, vehicles, or bank accounts to recover Lisa's debt. These assets are protected because they are owned by "Gourmet Catering," not by Lisa individually.

Instead, the creditors approached a court and requested an order to charge Lisa's interest in the partnership. If the court grants this order, the creditors will be entitled to receive Lisa's share of the profits from "Gourmet Catering." However, this does not make them partners in "Gourmet Catering." They have no say in the management or operations of the catering business and cannot make decisions affecting its day-to-day activities.

Furthermore, if Lisa were to pass away, her ownership in the partnership cannot be transferred through her will. Her share in "Gourmet Catering" remains with the partnership, and the agreement among the partners will dictate how her interest is to be handled posthumously.

6. Financial Rights and Bene-fits

6.1 Distribution of Capital and Profits – Equal Sharing

Unless specified otherwise in the partnership agreement, all partners' capital contributions and profits are divided equally. This means that even if the partners have invested different amounts of capital initially, they would still share profits equally unless there is a clause in the partnership agreement that dictates profit sharing in proportion to their capital contributions.

Therefore, if partners desire a distribution system based on their respective investments, this must be clearly outlined in the partnership agreement.

Consider a scenario with a new bakery, "Sweet Treats," founded by three partners: Emma, Sarah, and Liam. They decide to start their business with the following capital contributions: Emma invests £15,000, Sarah contributes £10,000, and Liam puts in £5,000. Their partnership agreement, however, does not specify how profits will be divided.

In this case, according to standard partnership rules, despite their unequal capital contributions, all three partners – Emma, Sarah, and Liam – are entitled to an equal share of the profits from "Sweet Treats." This means that regardless of whether Emma contributes the most or Liam the least, each will receive an equal portion of the profits.

If Emma, Sarah, and Liam want the profit distribution to reflect their respective capital contributions, they must explicitly state this in their partnership agreement.

For instance, they could agree that profits will be divided in the same ratio as their initial investments, meaning Emma receives 50%, Sarah 33.3%, and Liam 16.7% of the profits. This proportional distribution, however, must be detailed in the partnership agreement to be enforceable.

(a) **Restrictions on Profit Distribution Before Dissolution.** Within a partnership, partners are not entitled to any distribution of the firm's profits or capital before the dissolution of the partnership unless there is a mutual agreement among the partners that stipulates otherwise.

This means that the standard practice is to retain profits within the business until the partnership is dissolved or as specified in an agreement.

Consider "ABC Consulting," a partnership with three partners: Anne, Brian, and Carlos. The partnership is thriving, and profits are increasing.

Despite the success, Anne wants to withdraw some profits for personal use. However, the partnership agreement of "ABC Consulting" does not specify any distribution of earnings before the dissolution of the partnership.

Therefore, Anne cannot unilaterally decide to withdraw profits. Anne can legally start her share if Anne, Brian, and Carlos collectively agree to distribute profits before the dissolution.

(b) **Transferability of Profit Share.** While a partner's entitlement to a share of the partnership's profits can be transferred or assigned to another party, such an assignment does not grant the assignee any rights to participate in the management or decision-making of the firm.

Additionally, the assignee does not inherit any liability for the firm's obligations through this assignment. For an assignee to become a full partner, with management participation and liability for obligations, the consent of all existing partners is required unless the partnership agreement has provisions that state otherwise.

Carlos, from "ABC Consulting," decides to assign his profit share to his friend, David, as he plans to semi-retire. David now has a right to Carlos's share of the profits, but this assignment does not grant David any rights to participate in managing "ABC Consulting."

Also, David is not liable for any debts or obligations of the partnership. To be involved in the partnership's management and share in its liabilities, all partners, Anne, Brian, and Carlos, would need to agree to make David a full partner, or such a provision should already exist in the partnership agreement.

6.2 Allocation of Losses in a Partnership

In a typical partnership arrangement, the partners must share the partnership's losses equally, mirroring the division of profits. This includes losses related to capital or other aspects of the partnership's operations.

However, if the partnership agreement specifies a different arrangement for the distribution of profits, then, upon dissolution, the partners will bear any remaining losses in the same ratio as their profit-sharing arrangement.

In essence, how profits are divided in the partnership agreement also dictates the proportion in which losses will be shared unless explicitly stated otherwise.

Imagine a partnership, "GreenTech Innovations," formed by three partners: Zoe, Max, and Lily. Their partnership agreement states that profits are to be shared as follows: Zoe receives 50%, Max receives 30%, and Lily gets 20%, based on their varying levels of investment and expertise.

If "GreenTech Innovations" incurs losses, these are initially presumed to be shared equally among Zoe, Max, and Lily. This is the standard practice without a specific provision regarding losses in the partnership agreement.

However, since their partnership agreement specifies an unequal distribution of profits, the losses will be shared similarly if the partnership dissolves. Therefore, upon dissolution, Zoe would be responsible for 50% of the losses, Max for 30%, and Lily for 20%.

This arrangement ensures that the distribution of losses aligns with the agreed-upon profit-sharing ratios, maintaining equitable financial responsibility among the partners.

6.3 Record Keeping in Partnerships

Partners must maintain accurate financial records due to the complexity of managing profits, losses, and other financial responsibilities. These records, or partnership books, must be kept at the firm's primary place of business, accessible to every partner. Each partner has the right to examine and replicate these records to understand their financial entitlements and obligations within the partnership.

In "City Constructions," a building partnership, all financial transactions are recorded in the partnership books kept at their main office. Partner Jane regularly reviews these records to track her share of profits, her contribution to any losses, and other financial commitments.

6.4 Interest on Capital and Loans

Partners are not entitled to earn interest on the capital they invest in the partnership. However, if a partner lends additional funds to the partnership, they are entitled to an interest payment on that loan at a rate of 5% per annum.

If Max, a partner in "Tech Solutions," lends £10,000 to the partnership, besides his initial capital contribution, he is entitled to annual interest of 5% on this loan amount.

6.5 Compensation for Work

Partners typically are not compensated for their work managing the partnership's business. However, a partnership agreement may specify that managing partners receive a salary for their managerial roles, differentiating them from 'sleeping' partners who solely invest and do not partake in daily operations.

"Creative Agency" has a partnership agreement stating that Sarah, who manages daily operations, receives a salary, while John, an investor partner, does not engage in management and, thus, does not receive a salary.

6.6 Indemnification

The Partnership Act mandates that partnerships indemnify partners for any expenses or liabilities incurred while conducting partnership business or preserving the partnership's business or property.

If Lily, a partner at "Lily's Florist," purchases flowers on behalf of the partnership or incurs expenses in maintaining the shop, the partnership must reimburse her for these expenditures.

7. Administration of the Partnership

Under the guidelines of the Partnership Act, each partner is granted an equal opportunity to participate in the management of the partnership's business. Like others in the Act, this principle can be altered by mutual consent among the partners.

It's typical for a partnership agreement to delineate varying degrees of involvement for each partner, from active managerial roles to passive, investment-focused positions, known as 'sleeping partners.' Without specific stipulations in the partnership agreement, the standard practice is to adhere to the principle of 'one partner, one vote,' ensuring equal managerial input from all partners.

In a design firm "Vertex Creations," the partnership agreement specifies different management roles. Rachel and Tom, the founding partners, are actively involved in day-to-day operations and decision-making.

Meanwhile, Sean, a third partner, is designated as a sleeping partner; he has invested capital but needs to be more engaged in the regular management of the firm.

In this setup, Rachel and Tom handle the managerial aspects, while Sean's role is limited to investment contributions, aligning with the terms of their partnership agreement. Each would have an equal say in management decisions without such a specified arrangement.

7.1 Consensus on Partnership Decisions

In general, the governance of a partnership is guided by the principle of simple majority voting for management decisions. This is the default approach unless the partnership agreement specifies a different method for decision-making.

Nonetheless, specific key actions within a partnership necessitate the unanimous consent of all current partners, regardless of the usual voting procedure.

These actions include:

(a) The **introduction** of a new partner into the partnership,

(b) Any **significant change** to the nature or type of business conducted by the partnership,

(c) **Modifications** to the terms of the partnership agreement.

It's also important to note that a partner can only be expelled from the partnership by a majority vote if an explicit provision in the partnership agreement allows for such an action and all partners have agreed upon it.

In a law firm, "Legal Eagles," consisting of four partners, a decision to invest in new legal software can be made by a simple majority vote.

However, if they want to start offering a new type of legal service, representing a change like their business, or if they wish to amend their partnership agreement, all four partners must agree unanimously.

Additionally, if the partners want to admit a new lawyer into the partnership, this also requires the unanimous agreement of all existing partners.

8. Responsibilities Among Partners

8.1 Fiduciary Duty

In a partnership, common law imposes a fiduciary duty upon the partners. This duty obligates them to act in good faith and prioritise the partnership's interests. A fiduciary relationship is characterised by high trust and confidence, expecting partners to put the partnership's interests above their own.

In a marketing firm, "Bright Ideas Partnership," Liam, one of the partners, learns about a lucrative opportunity for the firm. Instead of sharing this information with his partners, he secretly negotiates a deal for his benefit.

This action breaches his fiduciary duty to act in the best interests of "Bright Ideas Partnership" and to maintain trust and confidence with his partners.

8.2 Obligation to Share Information

Partners must disclose all relevant Information concerning the partnership to their fellow partners or legal representatives. This duty ensures transparency and informed decision-making within the partnership.

Sarah, a partner in "Sunrise Catering," discovers a potential health violation in their kitchen operations. She must inform her partners immediately about this issue, even if she believes she can resolve it independently. She ensures that all partners know significant matters affecting the partnership by doing so.

8.3 Responsibility to Account for Undisclosed Profits

A partner must report and hand over to the partnership any profits or benefits they acquire independently in transactions related to the partnership or through the use of partnership assets or the partnership name without the other partners' consent. This includes gains from business opportunities due to their association with the partnership.

Alex, a partner in "TechGear," a technology consulting firm, is approached by a firm client to work on a private project. He completed the project outside of "TechGear" and received payment. As this business came to him through his involvement with the partnership, he must report and transfer these earnings to "TechGear."

(a) **Profits from Competing Business.** Suppose a partner engages in a business that competes with the partnership without the other partners' approval. In that case, they must account for and transfer all profits from that competing business to the partnership. This rule prevents partners from unfairly benefiting at the expense of the partnership.

Emily, a partner in "EcoSolutions," a green technology firm, started her own side business in solar panel installations, directly competing with "EcoSolutions." Even if Emily's business is booming, she must disclose and hand over the profits from this venture to "EcoSolutions," as her competing business could potentially harm the partnership's interests.

9. Ending of the Partnership

Unlike corporations or LLPs, a general partnership is not designed to last indefinitely. It ceases to exist as it originally stood when there's a change in the composition of partners. While the business may continue, technically, a new partnership is formed when there's a change in membership.

Dissolution Methods:

9.1 Ending Without Court Involvement

(a) **Expiration of Term:** If the partnership agreement specifies a duration or a specific project, the partnership dissolves at the end of that term or upon project completion. If a partner paid a premium for a fixed-term partnership and it ends early (except due to a partner's death), the court may order a partial refund.

"Seasonal Events Ltd.," a partnership formed to organise a series of summer festivals, dissolves automatically after the last festival, as agreed in the partnership terms.

(b)   **Ending a Partnership at Will through Notice.**
In partnerships not established for a specific duration (referred to as 'partnership at will'), any partner
can terminate the partnership simply by notifying
the other partners of their intention. The partnership will officially dissolve on the date specified in
the notice or, if no specific date is mentioned when
the notice is communicated to the other partners.
This process allows for a relatively straightforward
dissolution mechanism in flexible partnership arrangements not bound by a fixed term.

In a partnership, "City Bakery," without a fixed term, if partner
Amy decides to leave, she can dissolve the partnership by
giving notice to her partners, James and Sue.

(c)   **Bankruptcy, Death, or Charge:** The partnership ends upon a partner's death, bankruptcy, or if a
partner's share is charged for their debt, and the remaining partners choose to dissolve it.

If "City Bakery's" James becomes bankrupt, the partnership
can be dissolved.

(d)   **Termination Arising from Illegality.** A partnership is automatically dissolved if a situation
renders the continuation of its business or the operation of the alliance itself illegal. This could be due
to changes in laws or regulations that make the
partnership's business activities unlawful. This cause
for dissolution is distinct because it is not subject to

alteration or exception through terms in the partnership agreement. When legality becomes an issue, the partnership must cease operations, regardless of any previous agreements or arrangements among the partners.

9.2 Ending a Partnership through Court Intervention

Under certain circumstances, a partnership may be dissolved through a court order, as outlined in both the Mental Capacity Act 2005 and the Partnership Act.

This legal intervention can occur in the following situations:

(a) **Dissolution Due to Permanent Incapacity.** When a partner in a partnership becomes permanently unable to fulfil their obligations under the partnership contract, the remaining partners have the legal right to seek a partnership dissolution through a court order. This provision addresses cases where a partner's incapacity significantly impedes the partnership's ability to operate effectively and fulfil its objectives.

In "Fine Dining Co.," a culinary partnership, one of the partners, Chef Marco, unfortunately, suffers a long-term illness that renders him unable to continue his duties in the kitchen or participate in the management of the restaurant. Given Chef Marco's crucial role and his inability to contribute to the partnership, the other partners, after considering all options, decide to apply for a court-ordered dissolution of "Fine Dining Co." due to his permanent incapacity.

(b) **Harmful Conduct:** This situation arises when a partner's actions negatively impact the operation and reputation of the partnership in a way that is detrimental to the business. If a partner's conduct is significantly harmful, considering the specific nature of the business, another partner has the right to seek a court-ordered dissolution of the partnership.

In "TechForward Partners," a software development company, one of the partners, Alex, is found to be involved in embezzling funds from the company.

This illegal activity damages the partnership's financial standing and tarnishes its reputation in the industry. Given the severe nature of the misconduct and its adverse effects on the business, the other partners, Julia and Sam, decide to file for a court-ordered dissolution of the partnership, citing Alex's prejudicial conduct as the primary reason.

This action is taken to protect the business's remaining assets and dissociate from the implicated partner's unethical practices.

(c) **Repeated Violations of the Partnership Agreement:** Suppose a partner consistently or deliberately breaches the partnership agreement or acts in a way that makes continued partnership operation impractical (such as repeated breaches of trust). In that case, other partners can apply for dissolution through the court.

In "City Construction Partners," Mike repeatedly violates the partnership agreement by making unauthorised financial decisions. Frustrated by his continual disregard for the agreed-upon terms, his partners seek a court-ordered dissolution due to his persistent breaches.

(d) **Unprofitability:** In line with the Partnership Act's definition of a profit-oriented partnership, if the business can only operate at a loss, the court may dissolve the partnership.

"Artisan Bakers," a partnership, has been operating at a loss for several years, with no prospect of turning a profit. The partners collectively decide to apply for dissolution through the court, as the business no longer fulfils the Partnership Act's criterion of operating 'with a view of profit.'

(e) **Just and Equitable Reasons:** The court may also dissolve a partnership if deemed just and equitable. This is often invoked in scenarios where partners are at an impasse or deadlock, unable to reconcile fundamental disagreements or differing visions for the partnership.

"Creative Minds Advertising," a partnership of three advertising experts, faces a major deadlock. Two partners, Alice and Bob, want to expand the business into digital marketing, while the third partner, Charles, insists on focusing solely on traditional media.

Despite numerous discussions and attempts at compromise, they are unable to reach an agreement. The disagreement starts affecting the firm's daily operations and strategic decisions. Recognising that this impasse is hindering the business's growth and operations, Alice and Bob decide to apply to the court for a dissolution of the partnership because it is equitable to do so. Their application is based on the fundamental differences in vision for the company's future, which they believe cannot be reconciled.

9.3 Consequences of Dissolution

(a) **Continued Authority of Partners.** Following the dissolution of a partnership, the partners maintain certain authorities and responsibilities. Despite the dissolution, partners continue to have the power to legally bind the firm for the specific purpose of winding up its affairs. This includes completing any business transactions initiated but not finalised before the dissolution. This continuation of authority is necessary to ensure an orderly and effective conclusion of the partnership's remaining business activities and obligations.

(b) **Allocation of Partnership Assets Post-Dissolution.** Upon the dissolution of a partnership, the process of distributing the partnership assets occurs in a specific order:

• Payment of Debts: Initially, the assets are used to settle any outstanding debts of the partnership. If these assets are insufficient to cover all debts, the partners become personally liable for the remaining amount.

• Repayment of Partner Advances: If, after paying all creditors, there are remaining assets, these are first used to repay any financial advances or loans made by the partners to the partnership.

• Return of Capital Contributions: Following the repayment of loans, any remaining assets are used to return the capital contributions made by the partners, assuming these have not already been reimbursed.

• Distribution of Remaining Assets: If assets are still left after all the above steps, these are divided among the partners. The division is based on the same proportion as profit sharing, typically equally unless specified otherwise in the partnership agreement.

10.Taxation of Partnerships and Partners

The taxation of individual partners in a partnership is regulated by the Income Tax Act 2007. Under this legislation, every partner must report their portion of the partnership's profit on their personal income tax return annually.

This is obligatory regardless of whether the profits were distributed to the partners or retained within the business. The reported income from the partnership will then be subject to income tax at the rate applicable to each partner's total income level. This ensures that each partner pays tax on their fair share of the profits generated by the partnership, aligned with their tax obligations.

Imagine "Riverdale Design," a partnership formed by three partners: Alice, Betty, and Charles. In the financial year, "Riverdale Design" made a profit of £150,000. The partnership agreement states that profits are to be shared equally among the three partners. Therefore, each partner's share of the profit is £50,000.

Under the Income Tax Act 2007:

- Alice, Betty, and Charles must each include £50,000 in their tax returns as personal income, representing their share of the partnership's profit for the year.

- This inclusion is necessary even if "Riverdale Design" decides to reinvest the profits into the business rather than distributing them.

- The £50,000 will be taxed according to each partner's income tax rate. For instance, if Alice falls into a higher tax bracket due to other income sources, her tax rate on the partnership income will be higher compared to Betty and Charles, who might be in a lower tax bracket.

This taxation structure ensures that each partner pays income tax on their rightful share of the partnership's profits by their overall income level.

CHAPTER 3. CHARAC-TERISTICS OF LIMITED LIABILITY PARTNER-SHIPS

An LLP combines elements of a limited company and a general partnership, offering a unique structure that provides its members with little liability protection, similar to that in a limited company while retaining the operational flexibility of a traditional partnership.

This structure is particularly advantageous for large professional groups, such as law firms and accounting practices, where the partners prefer not to have personal and unlimited liability for the business's debts yet desire the managerial flexibility that a partnership offers.

LLPs are regulated under the Limited Liability Partnerships Act 2000 (LLPA) and related legislation. This act lays out the framework for the formation, operation, and dissolution of LLPs, providing a legal structure that combines the benefits of limited liability for its members with the flexibility of partnership operations. This structure is especially beneficial for professionals who require flexibility in management without exposing their assets to the risks associated with the business's liabilities.

Consider "Cityscape Legal," an extensive legal practice. The founding members decided to structure their business as a Limited Liability Partnership (LLP). This decision is driven by their desire to protect their assets from the firm's liabilities while maintaining the flexibility in management that is typical of a traditional partnership.

As an LLP, "Cityscape Legal" is governed by the Limited Liability Partnerships Act 2000. This means each LLP member (or partner) is protected from personal liability for business debts or claims against the firm. For instance, if the LLP faces legal claims or incurs debts, the member's personal assets are safeguarded against these liabilities.

Despite this protection, "Cityscape Legal" operates like a traditional partnership. The members have the freedom to manage the firm as they see fit without the more rigid structure of a corporation. They can make decisions about the business, divide profits, and manage day-to-day operations in a way that aligns with their professional goals and client needs.

This structure is particularly beneficial for "Cityscape Legal," given the nature of legal practices where large claims might arise. It allows the members to focus on providing legal services without the risk of personal financial exposure due to the actions of the LLP.

1. Establishing a Limited Liability Partnership

Forming a Limited Liability Partnership (LLP) follows a process similar to incorporating a limited company, as outlined in the Limited Liability Partnerships Act 2000 (LLPA).

Essential steps in this process include:

(a) **Registration with the Registrar of Companies:** An LLP must be formally registered with the Registrar of Companies. This is a mandatory step that legitimises the LLP as a legal entity.

(b) **Certificate of Incorporation:** Similar to a limited company, an LLP is permitted to commence business activities once a certificate of incorporation has been issued. This certificate is a crucial document that officially acknowledges the existence of the LLP.

(c) **Unique Name and Identification:** An LLP must have a unique name used to identify it on the register of companies at Companies House. Additionally, it is assigned a company number, further distinguishing it as an individual legal entity.

(d) **Governance in the absence of an Agreement:** In situations where there is no formal LLP agreement among the members, the governance of the LLP defaults to the provisions set out in the LLPA. However, it is common in practice for members to draft an LLP agreement that specifically addresses the management and operational aspects of the partnership. Once in place, this agreement supersedes the statutory provisions of the LLPA, allowing for tailored governance suited to the member's specific needs and circumstances.

Drafting an LLP agreement is a practical step typically undertaken by the members to ensure clarity in the management, profit sharing, responsibilities, and other critical aspects of the LLP's operations.

Documentation for LLP Incorporation:

Specific information must be provided in the incorporation documents to incorporate a Limited Liability Partnership (LLP).

This includes:

(a) **LLP Name:** The chosen name for the LLP must include 'LLP' or 'Limited Liability Partnership' at the end to indicate its legal structure.

(b) **Registered Office:** The location and address of the LLP's registered office. This address serves as the official address for legal correspondence.

(c) **Member Details:** Information about the members of the LLP, including their names and addresses. An LLP must have at least two designated members responsible for compliance with statutory obligations.

(d) **Persons with Significant Control:** If applicable, details of any individuals who have significant control over the LLP. This could include individuals with a substantial share of voting rights or the power to appoint or remove the majority of the board members.

2. Independent Legal Identity of an LLP

Like a limited company, an LLP possesses its own separate legal personality distinct from its individual members.

This independent legal status confers **several significant characteristics:**

(a) **Ownership of Property:** The LLP can own property in its name rather than in the names of its members.

(b) **Contractual Agreements:** Contracts are made and executed in the name of the LLP, not under the members' names. This Arrangement allows the LLP to engage in legal and business transactions as its entity.

(c) **Legal Actions:** The LLP can initiate or defend legal action in its name. This means that any legal proceedings are directed at the LLP as an entity rather than its members.

(d) **Perpetual Succession:** One of the critical distinctions from a general partnership is that an LLP enjoys endless succession. This means that the LLP continues to exist regardless of changes in membership. A member's departure, death, or bankruptcy does not affect the LLP's continuous existence. This perpetual succession ensures stability and continuity for the LLP, making it an attractive structure for businesses looking for longevity and resilience in their operational framework.

3. Rights and Responsibilities of LLP Members

3.1 Minimum Membership Requirement

Every Limited Liability Partnership (LLP) must have at least two members at all times. In cases where an LLP continues its business operations with only one member for a period extending beyond six months, the sole member during that period assumes a significant financial risk.

This individual becomes jointly and severally liable with the LLP for any debts incurred by the LLP after the first six months of being a single-member entity. This liability extends throughout the duration when the LLP operates with just one member, emphasising the importance of maintaining the minimum membership requirement to protect individual members against extensive personal financial obligations.

Consider "Innovate Tech LLP," which was initially established with three members: Amy, Brian, and Charles. However, due to unforeseen circumstances, Brian and Charles decide to leave the partnership, leaving Amy as the sole member.

During the first six months of operating "Innovate Tech LLP" alone, Amy is protected by the limited liability status of the LLP. The debts incurred during this period are the responsibility of the LLP, not Amy personally.

However, if Amy continues to run the business as the only member beyond six months, she faces increased financial risk. From the start of the seventh month, any new debts or financial obligations incurred by "Innovate Tech LLP" become a personal liability for Amy. She and the LLP are held jointly and severally liable for these debts. This means creditors can pursue Amy personally for repayment if the LLP's assets are insufficient to cover these obligations.

To avoid this personal liability, Amy must ensure that "Innovate Tech LLP" either ceases operations or brings in at least one additional member before the six-month mark of her being the sole member.

(a) **Consent for New Members.** Initially, the members of an LLP are those individuals who sign the incorporation documents. If the LLP wishes to add new members later, unanimous consent from all current members is typically required unless the LLP agreement stipulates a different process. This requirement ensures that all existing members agree to introduce new partners into the business.

(b) **Role of Designated Members.** Designated members in an LLP are responsible for specific administrative and compliance tasks.

Their duties include:

- We are appointing and removing auditors.

- I am submitting annual confirmation statements to Companies House.

- She was signing and filing the LLP's accounts.

- We are ensuring compliance with statutory filing requirements, such as registering documents and notifying Companies House of changes in membership.

- In cases where an LLP does not explicitly appoint designated members, all members are legally treated as designated members and share these responsibilities.

(c) **Notification of Changes.** An LLP must inform the Registrar of Companies about any changes in its membership or designated members within 14 days of the occurrence of these changes. This includes the addition of new members and the departure of existing ones. Failure to adhere to this reporting requirement constitutes an offence and can lead to legal repercussions for the LLP. This rule ensures a clear and up-to-date record of who is responsible for the management and obligations of the LLP.

3.2 Agency and Authority of LLP Members

In a Limited Liability Partnership (LLP), as in a general partnership, each member acts as an agent of the LLP.

This agency role comes with specific responsibilities and powers:

(a) **Duty of Care:** Members are obligated to act with a duty of care towards the LLP, ensuring their actions align with the partnership's best interests.

(b) **Binding the LLP in Contracts:** Members have the authority to enter into contracts on behalf of the LLP, provided they act within their actual or apparent authority.

(c) **Liability in Tort:** If a member acts within their actual or apparent authority, they can also make the LLP liable in tort (a civil wrong, such as negligence).

However, there are **limitations to this agency role**, similar to those in a general partnership:

(a) **Limitation of Authority:** If a member acts without the necessary authority, and the third party they are dealing with is aware that the member lacks authority or does not know or believe that the individual is a member of the LLP, then the LLP is not bound by the member's actions. This limitation protects the LLP from unauthorised actions by its members that could potentially harm the partnership.

Consider "TechVision LLP," a technology consulting firm with four members: Alice, Bob, Charlie, and Dana.

Duty of Care and Contractual Authority: Alice, acting as a member, negotiates and signs a contract with a new client for a large project. Because she is acting within her authority and for the benefit of "TechVision LLP," this contract is binding on the LLP. Alice's actions also reflect her duty of care towards the LLP in securing beneficial business.

Liability in Tort: Charlie, while working on a client project, accidentally breached client confidentiality, a tort of negligence. Since Charlie acted within his apparent authority for "TechVision LLP," the LLP could be held liable for this tortious action.

Limitation of Authority: without consulting the other members, Bob unilaterally decides to enter into a high-risk investment using LLP's funds. Dana, another member, learned about this and informed the investment firm that Bob did not have the authority to make this investment on behalf of "TechVision LLP."

Additionally, the investment firm was aware that Bob's actions were outside the usual scope of business for the LLP. In this case, the investment firm cannot hold "TechVision LLP" accountable for Bob's unauthorised action, thus protecting the LLP from potential financial harm due to Bob's overreach.

3.3 Register of People with Significant Control in LLPs

Like limited companies, Limited Liability Partnerships (LLPs) must maintain a register of People with Significant Control (PSCs).

A PSC in an LLP is defined as an individual who meets any of the **following criteria**:

(a) **Ownership of Assets upon Dissolution:** Holds, directly or indirectly, rights over more than 25% of the LLP's assets in the event of winding up.

(b) **Voting Rights:** Possesses, directly or indirectly, more than 25% of the voting rights on matters that require a decision by the members of the LLP.

(c) **Management Control:** Has the right, directly or indirectly, to appoint or remove the majority of those involved in the management of the LLP.

(d) **Influence or Control:** Exercises significant influence or control over a trust or firm (which isn't a legal entity) that meets any other conditions mentioned above about the LLP.

Members of the LLP should carefully examine their LLP agreement to identify any individuals who might meet these criteria. Identifying PSCs is crucial for compliance with legal requirements and for maintaining transparency in the management and control of the LLP. The register of PSCs is a key document that provides clarity on who has significant control or influence over the LLP, and it must be kept updated with accurate information.

Consider "Vertex Architects LLP," an LLP with three members: Rachel, Tom, and Sarah. The "Vertex Architects" LLP agreement does not specify a unique profit-sharing arrangement.

Therefore, by default, Rachel, Tom, and Sarah are entitled to an equal share of both the capital and the profits of the LLP.

Equal Profit Sharing: Suppose "Vertex Architects LLP" earns a profit of £300,000 in a financial year. Without a profit-sharing clause in the LLP agreement, this profit is divided equally among the three members. Each member, Rachel, Tom, and Sarah, receives £100,000 as their share of the profits.

No Remuneration for Management Roles: Rachel, who is more involved in the management aspect of the LLP, and Tom, who primarily focuses on architectural design, are not entitled to any additional remuneration for their work in the business. Their financial compensation is limited to their share of the profits. This is in contrast to a corporate structure, where individuals might receive salaries for their roles in addition to profit shares.

This example illustrates the typical approach to profit distribution in an LLP, emphasising the equal sharing of profits and the lack of remuneration for management roles unless otherwise specified in the LLP agreement.

3.4 Entitlement to Profits in an LLP

In the absence of any specific terms in the LLP agreement that state otherwise, members of a Limited Liability Partnership (LLP) have the right to an equal share in both the capital and profits of the LLP. This standard arrangement ensures that unless there is a clear agreement outlining a different profit-sharing structure, all members benefit equally from the success of the LLP.

Additionally, similar to the rules in a general partnership, members of an LLP are typically not entitled to receive remuneration for their roles in conducting the business or managing the LLP. This means that members are not paid salaries or wages for their work within the LLP. Instead, their financial compensation is derived from their share of the profits. This principle emphasises the collective responsibility and benefit-sharing model inherent in the LLP structure, where the rewards of the business's success are distributed as profits rather than as salaries or wages for work done.

3.5 Member Indemnification in an LLP

Similar to the provisions in a general partnership, a Limited Liability Partnership (LLP) must indemnify its members for expenses and liabilities they incur while conducting the LLP's business or in actions taken to preserve the business or its assets. This indemnification means that if a member of the LLP incurs costs or assumes financial liabilities while acting in the interest of the LLP, they are entitled to reimbursement or compensation from the LLP.

In "Digital Innovations LLP," a technology consultancy, one of the members, Emma, purchases new software for the firm and travels to a conference to secure potential clients, incurring substantial expenses. Emma's actions were for the benefit of "Digital Innovations LLP" and in line with its business activities, so she is entitled to be indemnified by the LLP.

This indemnification would cover the costs of the software and her travel expenses, as these were necessary expenditures to conduct and preserve the LLP's business. Emma would submit these expenses to the LLP, which would then reimburse her, ensuring that she is not personally financially disadvantaged for her contributions to the business.

3.6 Access to Books and Records in an LLP

In line with the practices of a general partnership, members of a Limited Liability Partnership (LLP) have the right to access and review the LLP's books and records at any time. This entitlement ensures transparency within the LLP and allows members to stay informed about the partnership's financial status and operational activities.

In "EcoSolutions LLP," an environmental consultancy, each member, including John, Lisa, and Mohammed, has the right to inspect the financial records, client contracts, and other essential documents of the LLP. Suppose John wants to assess the financial health of the LLP or understand the details of a new client contract. He can request access to the relevant books and records and is entitled to review these documents at his discretion.

This access enables John and the other members to make informed decisions about the LLP's operations, investments, and strategy, contributing to a transparent and collaborative management environment.

3.7 Management of an LLP

In a Limited Liability Partnership (LLP), like a general partnership, each member has the right to participate in the management of the LLP unless an agreement specifies otherwise. This means that every member is entitled to have a say in the day-to-day management and decision-making processes of the LLP. A majority vote of the members can typically make decisions about 'ordinary' business matters.

However, all members' consent is required for significant decisions, particularly those that would alter the LLP's business's fundamental nature. This provision ensures that substantial changes to the LLP's business direction or strategy are made collaboratively and unanimously among all members.

In "Creative Design LLP," a graphic design firm, the management and operational decisions are usually made through a majority vote among its members - Ava, Ben, and Carlos. For instance, decisions about purchasing new design software or hiring additional staff are made based on a majority vote.

However, if Ava proposes to expand the business into web development, which represents a significant shift from the LLP's core focus on graphic design, this would require the approval of both Ben and Carlos. This change, like the business, needs unanimous consent from all members, ensuring that such a pivotal decision is agreed upon by everyone involved.

3.8 Responsibility for Competing Business and Personal Benefit

In a Limited Liability Partnership (LLP), similar to a general partnership, there are **specific duties** regarding competition and personal benefits:

(a) **Competition with the LLP:** If a member engages in a business that competes with the LLP without obtaining the LLP's consent, they must turn over all profits from that competing business to the LLP. This rule is designed to prevent members from unfairly benefiting at the expense of the LLP.

(b) **Personal Benefit from LLP Transactions:** Members must also account for and potentially reimburse the LLP for any unique benefits they gain from transactions related to the LLP or through the use of the LLP's property, name, or business connections unless such benefits were obtained with the consent of the LLP.

3.9 Liability for Member Actions

(a) **Liability Among Members:** Generally, individual members of an LLP are not personally liable for the wrongful acts or omissions of other members committed during the LLP's business or with the authority of the LLP. This limited liability feature is one of the key benefits of operating under an LLP structure.

(b) **LLP's Liability:** While individual members may not be personally liable, the LLP itself is responsible to the same extent as the member who committed the wrongful act. This means that legal claims or debts arising from a member's wrongful actions fall upon the LLP rather than individual members' responsibility.

4. Public Disclosure Require-ments for LLPs

Limited Liability Partnerships (LLPs), enjoying the advantage of limited liability, are subject to more rigorous public disclosure and filing obligations akin to those of limited companies.

These **requirements**, aimed at maintaining transparency and accountability, **include submitting various documents to the Registrar of Companies:**

(a) **Annual Accounts:** An LLP must file its financial statements annually. These accounts clearly show the LLP's financial health and performance over the financial year.

(b) **Annual Confirmation Statement:** This yearly statement either confirms or updates the information about the LLP that is already on file with Companies House. It ensures that the public record remains accurate and current.

(c) **Appointments and Removals of Members:** Any changes in the membership of the LLP, such as new members joining or existing members leaving, must be reported.

(d) **Updates to Members' Details:** If there are any changes to the member's personal details, such as changes in names or addresses, these must also be filed.

(e) **Changes in Registered Name or Office:** Should the LLP change its official name or the address of its registered office, this information must be updated with the Registrar of Companies.

These filing requirements provide a level of oversight and transparency to external parties, such as creditors, clients, and regulatory bodies, regarding the operations and status of the LLP.

5. Financial Responsibilities in an LLP

5.1 Limited Liability of Members

In an LLP, members are not personally liable for the LLP's debts, reflecting its status as a separate legal entity, much like a limited company. The extent of a member's financial liability is limited to their capital contribution.

This is a crucial distinction between LLPs and general partnerships. Upon the winding up of an LLP, a member is only required to contribute to the LLP's assets as outlined in the LLP agreement. If members have fully paid their capital contribution and the LLP agreement does not mandate further contributions, they have no additional financial obligations towards the LLP's debts.

5.2 Personal Liability for Wrongful Actions

Like directors and shareholders of a limited company, members of an LLP are subject to the wrongful and fraudulent trading rules under the Insolvency Act 1986.

These rules can impose personal liability on members who engage in illegal or fraudulent activities, making them personally accountable for the LLP's debts in insolvency cases.

Clawback Provisions:

The law also includes provisions for clawback in the event of insolvent liquidation. Suppose a member withdraws assets from the LLP (such as profits, salaries, loan repayments, or other forms of property) within two years before the LLP enters insolvent liquidation, and they knew or should have reasonably known that such withdrawal would render the LLP unable to pay its debts.

In that case, the court may order them to return those assets to the LLP. This provision is designed to prevent members from extracting assets to the detriment of creditors in situations where the LLP is financially unstable.

6. Ending of an LLP

6.1 Voluntary Striking Off and Dissolution

An LLP can be voluntarily struck off the register and dissolved by its members for various reasons, such as if it is no longer active, required, or dormant. Most members can apply to the Registrar of Companies for this action.

Additionally, the Registrar can initiate striking off if there's evidence that the LLP is not operational, such as non-compliance with filing requirements or undelivered documents to the registered office.

This process is distinct from formal insolvency proceedings, which are more structured and creditor-focused.

(a) **Restrictions on Striking Off.** An LLP cannot be struck off if:

- It has engaged in trading or business activities within the last three months.

- It has changed its name within the previous three months.

- It is undergoing any form of insolvency proceedings.

(b) Notification Requirements:

- When applying for striking off, members must inform all relevant parties, including other members, creditors, employees, and pension fund trustees.

- Upon receiving a strike-off application, the Registrar will publish a notice in the London Gazette, allowing objections from interested parties. If no objections are raised, the LLP is struck off and dissolved three months after the notice's publication date.

6.2 Insolvency Procedures

An LLP can undergo insolvency through various means, similar to a limited company. **These include:**

(a) **Liquidation:** Both voluntary and compulsory liquidation processes are available for an LLP. In these procedures, assets are sold off to pay debts.

(b) **Administration:** An LLP can enter administration, where an administrator is appointed to oversee the business's affairs to repay creditors as much as possible.

(c) **Voluntary Arrangement** involves an agreement between the LLP and its creditors to pay off debts, often at a reduced rate or over a more extended period.

(d) **Receivership:** Secured creditors may appoint a receiver or administrative receiver to manage the LLP's assets, usually to recover the amount owed.

These insolvency options provide structured ways to address an LLP's financial difficulties while considering the interests of creditors and other stakeholders.

7. Taxation of LLPs and Their Members

The taxation structure for Limited Liability Partnerships (LLPs) **differs notably** from that of limited companies:

(a) **LLP Not Taxed as a Separate Entity:** Despite being recognised as a separate legal entity, an LLP is not subject to corporation tax. This contrasts with limited companies, which are taxed directly on their profits.

(b) **Taxation of Individual Members:** Instead, the members of an LLP are taxed individually on their income, much like partners in a general partnership. Each member must report their share of the LLP's profits on their tax returns and pay income tax accordingly.

(c) **Capital Gains Tax:** When it comes to the disposal of assets held by the LLP, members are individually liable for capital gains tax on their respective shares of any gains realised.

(d) **Inheritance Tax:** For inheritance tax purposes, the members of an LLP are treated in the same manner as partners in a general partnership. This means that their interests in the LLP may be considered part of their estate for inheritance tax calculations.

This taxation approach reflects the hybrid nature of LLPs, combining corporate structure elements with the tax treatment of a traditional partnership.

It allows for the legal benefits of limited liability while maintaining a pass-through taxation model where the tax obligations are borne by the individual members rather than the entity itself.

7.1 Exemption from Stamp Duty Land Tax for LLPs

In the context of property transfers to a Limited Liability Partnership (LLP), there is a notable exception regarding stamp duty land tax, particularly within the first year of the LLP's incorporation.

This exemption is applicable under specific conditions:

(a) **Property Transfer Requirements:** The property must be transferred to the LLP by:

- A person who is or was a partner in a partnership with the same members as the LLP.

- A person who holds the property as a bare trustee for a partner in such a partnership.

(b) **Consistency in Ownership Proportions:** The exemption is valid only if the proportional ownership of the transferred property within the LLP mirrors the proportional ownership in the original partnership. This means that the ownership stakes in the property should remain unchanged in the transition from the alliance to the LLP.

This stamp duty land tax exemption is significant as it facilitates the transition of assets from a general partnership structure to an LLP without incurring additional tax liabilities on property transfers. It is especially beneficial in restructuring scenarios where a partnership evolves into an LLP while retaining the same members and property ownership proportions.

CHAPTER 4. THE ESSENCE AND ESTABLISHMENT OF COMPANIES

1. Varieties of Registered Companies

Following English legal requirements, every company must undergo registration with the Registrar of Companies.

This registration classifies companies into various categories, each with its legal characteristics and operational guidelines. Recognising the unique aspects of each type of registered company is essential for comprehending their respective legal and business implications.

This knowledge is critical for those involved in creating, managing, or legally handling such entities, ensuring informed decision-making and compliance with regulatory standards.

1.1 Characteristics of Unlimited Companies

Unlimited companies, while uncommon, represent a unique corporate form. In these entities, the members bear personal liability for all the company's debts, akin to the liability faced by partners in a general partnership or sole proprietors.

One of the notable advantages of an unlimited company, apart from its incorporation and the acquisition of a separate legal identity distinct from its members, is the exemption from the requirement to disclose its accounts publicly. This aspect grants unlimited companies a higher level of confidentiality in financial matters compared to limited companies.

The choice to operate as an unlimited company typically stems from a strategic decision to leverage this privacy advantage, despite the inherent risk of unlimited personal liability for company debts.

1.2 Types of Limited Companies

A limited company is characterised by limiting its owners' (referred to as members) liability. There are two primary forms of limited companies: those limited by guarantee and those limited by shares.

(a) **Companies Limited by Guarantee.** This structure requires members to commit a predetermined amount (often a nominal sum like £1) in case of the company's liquidation. Predominantly adopted by non-profit organisations, such as charities, this model doesn't necessitate substantial capital investment from its members for operational viability. There are no shareholders in this setup, but there must be at least one member or guarantor.

"City Arts Trust," a non-profit organisation dedicated to promoting local arts, is a company limited by guarantee. Each member of the trust, such as local artists and art enthusiasts, has agreed to contribute £1 if the company is wound up. This structure suits "City Arts Trust" as it doesn't seek to generate profits for shareholders but aims to serve the community. This company has no shareholders; instead, it operates with members who support its artistic mission.

(b) **Companies Limited by Shares.** In this format, the members (also known as shareholders) are shielded from the company's debts beyond the value of their share investment. Once a shareholder has fully paid for their shares, which is typically the case, they bear no personal financial responsibility should the company face insolvency. Companies limited by shares are further categorised into private and public limited companies, each with specific operational and regulatory frameworks. These companies are the standard choice for businesses seeking investment through share capital while providing limited liability protection to their shareholders.

2. Distinction Between Private and Public Limited Companies

Companies limited by shares in the UK are bifurcated into private limited companies and public limited companies. This distinction has significant implications regarding their operations, registration requirements, and ability to issue shares.

2.1 Private Limited Companies (Ltd)

Private limited companies are the most frequently registered business entities at Companies House. These companies are typically the focus for newly qualified solicitors due to their prevalence and the nature of the legal work involved.

The defining characteristic of a private limited company is that it cannot offer its shares to the general public. Shares in such companies are usually owned by a small group of individuals and are traded or sold through private arrangements.

2.2 Public Limited Companies (PLCs)

Public limited companies, as opposed to private limited companies, can offer their shares to the public. Furthermore, if a PLC is listed, its shares can be traded on a stock exchange. A company must meet more stringent registration criteria to qualify as a PLC and engage in public trading.

Key among these is the requirement to have a minimum nominal share capital of £50,000 and to obtain a trading certificate. These additional regulations and requirements are in place to protect public investors and ensure the financial stability and transparency of the PLC.

The choice between operating as a private limited company or a PLC depends on various factors, including the scale of the business, its funding needs, and the desired level of regulatory scrutiny and public exposure.

3. Establishing a Company

3.1 Role of Promoters

A company, being a legal entity, exists only after registering at Companies House. The individuals who gather investors and manage the registration process are known as the company's 'promoters'.

While there isn't a specific statutory definition of a promoter, they are generally recognised as those who take active steps towards forming a company. It's important to note that professional advisors, like solicitors and accountants, do not classify as promoters merely by providing professional advice during the company formation process.

(a) **Creating the Memorandum of Association.** A vital responsibility of a promoter is to draft the Memorandum of Association. This document, authenticated by individuals intending to be company members, declares their intention to form the company and their agreement to become its members. The Memorandum of Association, along with the application for registration, needs to be submitted to the Registrar of Companies.

(b) **Fiduciary Duties of Promoters.** Similar to directors and partners, promoters are bound by fiduciary duties towards the company. These duties encompass acting in good faith and upholding the company's best interests. Promoters are required to disclose any personal gains or interests in transactions conducted on behalf of the company. They must also account for and potentially reimburse any profits from these transactions. This requirement is intended to prevent conflicts of interest and ensure that the actions of promoters are aligned with the company's objectives.

3.2 Pre-Incorporation Contracts

In establishing a company, promoters often engage in contractual arrangements before the company's formal registration. These arrangements, known as 'pre-incorporation contracts,' are crucial for setting up the operational framework of the company once it is officially registered and receives its certificate of incorporation.

Under both common law and the Companies Act 2006, **the following legal considerations apply to pre-incorporation contracts:**

(a) **Incapacity of the Yet-to-Be-Formed Company.** Since the company did not legally exist before its incorporation, it cannot be a contracting party. Contracts require at least two parties, and in the case of pre-incorporation contracts, the company itself cannot be one of them.

(b) **Personal Liability of Promoters.** Since the company cannot be a party to these contracts when they are made, promoters who enter into pre-incorporation contracts are personally liable for them. This means that promoters bear the responsibility for fulfilling these contractual obligations.

(c) **Continued Liability Post-Incorporation.** The personal liability of promoters on pre-incorporation contracts does not automatically cease upon the company's formation. The promoter remains personally responsible for these contracts even after the company is registered and begins operations.

(d) **Alteration of Liability.** Specific arrangements must be made to transfer the liability from the promoter to the company after its incorporation. This often involves a new contract where the company agrees to assume the obligations of the pre-incorporation contracts, effectively releasing the promoter from personal liability.

Understanding the implications of pre-incorporation contracts is essential for promoters to manage their risk and for the company to transition smoothly from formation to operational status.

3.3 Strategies for Promoters to Minimise Personal Liability

Promoters involved in the formation of a company can adopt several strategies to safeguard themselves from personal liability associated with pre-incorporation contracts:

(a) **Draft Contracts Pending Incorporation:** One of the simplest methods is to prepare the contract in draft form and delay its execution until the company has been formally incorporated. Once established, this approach ensures that the company becomes the contracting party, thereby avoiding personal liability for the promoter.

(b) **Novation Agreements:** Post-incorporation, promoters can enter into a novation agreement. This is a three-party contract involving the promoter, the newly formed company, and the external contracting party. The deal aims to substitute the company in place of the promoter in the pre-incorporation contract, releasing the promoter from any personal obligations under the original agreement.

(c) **Assignment and Indemnification Agreements:** Another protective measure is for the promoter to assign the benefits of the pre-incorporation contract to the company after it is incorporated. In exchange, the company agrees to indemnify the promoter against any liabilities arising from the contract. This means if the promoter is held liable, the company agrees to reimburse or compensate the promoter for those liabilities.

(d) **Utilising a Shelf Company:** To expedite the process and reduce the period during which a promoter might be liable, a promoter can incorporate a 'shelf company' – a pre-registered company with no activity or liabilities. This approach allows the promoter to engage in contracts shortly after acquiring the shelf company, thereby minimising the duration of personal liability exposure.

Each strategy offers a way to manage the risks associated with forming a new company, ensuring that the promoter is not unduly burdened with personal liability once the company begins its operations.

3.4 Utilising Shelf Companies

For promoters requiring swift incorporation, shelf companies present a viable solution. These are pre-formed entities with no prior trading history, often established by legal professionals. A promoter can acquire a shelf company and easily customise essential aspects, such as changing its members.

However, shelf companies are structured in a generic format and might be better for specific needs requiring customised articles of association.

3.5 Steps for Company Registration

To officially incorporate a company, promoters need to submit a series of documents to the Registrar of Companies at Companies House, **including:**

(a) **Proposed Company Name:** The intended name for the new company.

(b) **Registered Office Location:** The official address for communication and legal notices should be within the jurisdiction where the business operates. This is often the company's operational address or the address of the company's solicitor or accountant.

(c) **Business Activity and SIC Code:** A Standard Industrial Classification (SIC) code identifies the company's primary business activities.

(d) **Type of Company:** Indicating whether shares or guarantees will limit the company and whether it is a private or public entity.

(e) **Subscriber Details:** Information about the initial subscribers to the company's memorandum.

(f) **Statement of Capital and Initial Shareholdings:** Details on the company's initial capital structure and share distribution.

(g) **Proposed Officers:** Information about the individuals who will manage the company, including directors and, if applicable, the company secretary.

(h) **Persons with Significant Control:** Details of individuals with significant control over the company.

(i) **Compliance Statement:** A declaration of adherence to the requirements of the Companies Act 2006.

(j) **Registration Fee:** Payment of the applicable fee for registering the company.

These steps ensure that all relevant information is legally recorded and available, providing transparency and regulatory compliance from the outset of the company's existence.

3.6 Selection of a Company Name

When choosing a name for their company, promoters must adhere to **specific guidelines to ensure compliance with legal standards**:

(a) **Uniqueness:** The chosen name must differ from an existing company's name.

(b) **Suffix Requirement:** Depending on the type of company, the name must conclude with "Limited" or "Ltd" for private limited companies or "Public Limited Company" or "Plc" for public limited companies. In Wales, Welsh equivalents of these terms are acceptable.

(c) **Offensive Names:** Names deemed offensive are not permitted.

(d) **Government or Local Authority Association:** Any name implying a connection to government or local authorities requires prior approval.

(e) **Sensitive Words:** Names containing specific terms, like "Auditor," "Chartered," "Law Commission," or "Medical Centre," necessitate approval due to their sensitive nature.

Exception for Companies Limited by Guarantee:

These companies, often preferred by charities, are not obligated to include 'Limited' in their names, allowing for a less corporate public image.

3. 7 Procedure for Changing a Company Name

A company can alter its name after formation through either:

(a) **Special Resolution by Members:** This involves a formal decision made by a specified majority of the members.

(b) **Provisions in the Articles of Association:** If the company's articles allow for a name change, this can be another avenue for altering the company name.

Following a name change, the company must submit a copy of the resolution or a statement confirming the change following the articles to the Registrar of Companies.

Additionally, the company must formally notify the Registrar of the name change. This process ensures that the company's official records are up-to-date and reflect its current name.

3.8 Declaration of Share Capital and Initial Share Allotment

In the case of a company limited by shares, its Application for Registration with the Companies House must encompass detailed information about its share capital structure.

This includes:

(a) **Total Number of Shares:** The application must state the total number of shares to be held by the subscribers to the Memorandum of Association.

(b) **Aggregate Nominal Value of Shares:** This refers to the total face value of these shares. Typically, shares in private companies are assigned a nominal value, such as £1 per share. This nominal value represents the minimum price for each share that can be issued and should not be confused with the actual selling price of the shares, which can be higher. Directors must ensure that shares are not sold below this nominal value to avoid potential liability for breach of duty.

(c) **Share Classifications:** If the company's shares are categorised into different classes, each with distinct rights, these classes and their respective rights must be described in the application.

(d) **Paid-up and Unpaid Amounts on Shares:** The application should also include the amount of capital that shareholders will pay upon subscription (paid-up capital) and any portion of the share capital remaining unpaid.

3.9 Issuance of the Certificate of Incorporation

After the submission and examination of the registration documents by the Registrar of Companies, and provided that all the requirements are met satisfactorily, the next significant step in the formation of a company is the issuance of the Certificate of Incorporation. This document plays a crucial role in the establishment of a company:

(a) **Content of the Certificate:** The Certificate of Incorporation includes the company's unique registration number, which is vital for its legal identity.

(b) **Significance of the Certificate:** Often likened to a company's 'birth certificate', this document marks the official creation of the company. It confirms the company's existence under the law.

(c) **Legal Status and Trading Commencement:** The company is recognised as a legal entity from the date specified on the Certificate of Incorporation. From this date, the company is legally permitted to start its business operations and enjoy the benefits of limited liability.

4. The Constitution of a Company

The term 'constitution' in the context of a company, as referred to in the Companies Act 2006, encompasses a specific set of governing documents. A company's constitution primarily consists of its articles of association and any resolutions or agreements that members have adopted to modify these articles.

These documents collectively dictate the internal governance and operational framework of the company:

(a) **Articles of Association:** Every company is mandated to have articles of association, often simply referred to as 'articles'. These articles outline the company's internal management rules and cover various aspects like shareholders' rights, meetings' conduct, and directors' appointments.

(b) **Model Articles:** The Secretary of State has provided standard sets of model articles for different types of companies. These model articles automatically apply if a company does not submit its custom or amended articles to Companies House.

(c) **Bespoke Articles:** Companies can draft and submit their bespoke articles. This allows companies to tailor their governance structures to their specific needs as long as these bespoke articles comply with the law.

(d) **Focus on Private Companies Limited by Shares:** For this discussion, emphasis will be placed on the provisions of the Model Articles for Private Companies Limited by Shares, given their widespread adoption and relevance to most companies.

4.1 Key Elements in Articles of Association

The articles of association typically encompass:

(a) **Directorial Procedures:** Outlining the conduct of directors' meetings and decision-making.

(b) **Directorial Appointments and Removals:** Guidelines on how directors are appointed and removed.

(c) **Share Capital Handling:** Policies regarding issuing, allocating, and transferring shares.

(d) **Shareholder Rights:** Details about the rights attached to shares, such as voting and dividend entitlements.

(e) **Conduct of Shareholder Meetings:** Protocols for organising shareholder meetings, including notice requirements and quorum specifications.

BrightTech Ltd", a private limited company, has articles of association detailing that directors' meetings require a quorum of three directors and that a majority vote can make decisions. Their articles also outline the process for issuing new shares and set the voting rights for each share class.

4.2 Company's Purpose

(a) **Restricted Purposes:** Articles can define the company's objectives, such as "operating restaurants." Directors must comply with these restrictions or face legal repercussions, though actions beyond these objectives are still legally valid.

In its articles, EcoFood Ltd" states that its sole objective is to operate organic food stores. If the directors venture into clothing retail, they would act outside the company's stated objectives.

(b) **Unrestricted Purposes:** The absence of limitations in the articles allows the company to undertake any legal business activity. This broad scope is standard in model articles.

Innovate Inc.", a tech startup, has not specified any particular objective in its articles, allowing them to diversify into various tech sectors like software development, hardware manufacturing, or tech consultancy services.

4.3 Contractual Nature of Articles

The articles constitute a contract between the company and its shareholders and among the shareholders themselves, focusing primarily on membership-related rights.

"MediaWorks Ltd" shareholders rely on the company's articles to understand their dividend rights. When the company decides not to distribute dividends for one year, a shareholder refers to the articles to confirm their rights and the conditions under which dividends are paid.

4.4 Beyond the Articles: Shareholders' Agreements

In parallel to the articles, shareholders may form a shareholders' agreement, a private contract binding only its signatories. This can include specific clauses like unanimous decision-making for constitutional changes.

(a) **Amendment Constraints:** Under the Companies Act 2006, the company's constitution cannot mandate unanimous agreement for modifications; special resolutions suffice.

The "ArtGallery Ltd" shareholders enter into a separate shareholders' agreement that requires unanimous consent for any changes to the company's articles of association, offering additional protection to minority shareholders.

4.5 Modifying the Articles

Alterations to the articles require a special resolution and cannot impose new liabilities on shareholders, such as compulsory additional share purchases.

(a) Solidifying Provisions (Entrenchment):

- **Resolution Thresholds:** Ordinary resolutions need a simple majority, whereas special resolutions demand a minimum 75% majority.

- **Entrenchment Practices:** Provisions requiring more than a special resolution for changes can be entrenched in the articles.

- **Registrar Notification Requirement:** The Registrar must be informed of any entrenched provisions.

- **Prohibition on Total Amendment Restrictions:** While entrenchment can make amendments challenging, it cannot entirely prevent them; special resolutions remain a viable avenue for change.

GreenEnergy Ltd" has a provision in its articles that any changes to its environmental policies require approval by 90% of the shareholders, which is an example of an entrenched provision.

(b) Assessing Shareholders' Alterations. Alterations are typically assumed to be in the company's interest unless unreasonable. Shareholders not favouring an amendment can legally challenge it if it is not in the company's overall interest.

- **Protection of Minority Shareholders:** The impact on minority shareholders alone isn't grounds for a challenge unless the amendment discriminates against certain members, contrary to the company's collective interests.

FashionFiesta Ltd" has changed its articles to focus solely on sustainable fashion. A minority shareholder, believing this shift to be detrimental to the company's profitability, challenges the amendment in court. The court upholds the amendment, aligning it with the company's long-term interests and public image enhancement.

5. Separate Legal Personality of a Company

The principle of separate legal personality is one of the primary benefits of company incorporation. Under the law, an incorporated company is recognised as an independent legal entity, distinct from the individuals who are its members or who manage its operations. This separation affords the company **several key legal capabilities:**

(a) **Ownership of Assets:** The company can hold property and assets under its name, separate from its members.

(b) **Contractual Capacity:** It can enter into contracts independently, with the contractual obligations and rights being the company's own.

(c) **Financial Autonomy:** A company can borrow money, issue debt, and provide security for loans.

(d) **Independent Taxation:** The company is treated as a separate entity for tax purposes, meaning its profits are taxed independently of its members' income.

(e) **Legal Proceedings:** It can initiate or defend legal action under its name, distinct from the legal status of its members.

(f) **Perpetual Succession:** The company continues to exist even if the membership changes, ensuring business continuity beyond the involvement of its original or any specific members.

5.1 The Concept of the Corporate Veil in Limited Companies

The principle of separate legal personality in limited companies leads to the formation of what is often referred to as the 'veil of incorporation'.

This concept means that a limited company's members (shareholders) are not personally liable for the company's debts. This is a significant advantage over general partnerships, where members may face personal liability.

(a) **Piercing the Corporate Veil:** In certain exceptional cases, courts or laws may 'lift' or 'pierce' this corporate veil, making shareholders or directors personally liable for the company's obligations. **Instances where this might occur include:**

- **Fraud or Evasion:** If the company is established to perpetrate fraud or evade an existing debt, the veil of incorporation may be lifted to hold shareholders or directors personally accountable.

- **Breach of Contractual Clauses:** For example, if an employee forms a limited company to bypass a non-solicitation clause in their previous employment contract, the individual and the company could be liable for this breach.

- **Wrongful and Fraudulent Trading:** Directors may face personal liability if they knowingly involve the company in trading while insolvent. This could lead to civil or criminal charges, as discussed in the insolvency section.

- **Public Limited Companies and Trading Certificates:** Directors of a PLC can be personally liable for losses if the PLC engages in business activities without obtaining a required trading certificate.

- **Group Accounts:** In a corporate group, consolidated accounts might be necessary to recognise the link between companies. However, each company in the group maintains its liability; subsidiaries are not responsible for the debts of other subsidiaries or the parent company, nor is the parent company liable for the debts of its subsidiaries.

CHAPTER 5. CORPORATE LEADERSHIP: DIRECTORS AND OFFICERS

1. Role of Directors

A company's directors are vital officers responsible for managing its day-to-day affairs. Their role is pivotal in steering the company towards its strategic goals and ensuring its compliance with legal obligations.

(a) **Function Over Title:** Determining if someone functions as a director is more about their role and responsibilities within the company than their official title. This means assessing whether the individual makes significant decisions or has considerable influence over the company's operations.

(b) **Management and Decision-Making:** Directors make critical decisions about the company's business strategies, financial management, and operational procedures. They are expected to act in the company's best interests, balancing the needs of various stakeholders, including shareholders, employees, and customers.

(c) **Legal and Regulatory Compliance:** Directors must ensure the company adheres to all relevant laws and regulations. This includes financial reporting, employment laws, and industry-specific regulations.

(d) **Board Meetings and Corporate Governance:**
Directors typically operate collectively through
board meetings, discussing and making decisions on
important company matters. Their actions should
align with good corporate governance practices,
promoting transparency, fairness, and accountability
within the company.

1.2 Different Categories of Company Directors

(a) **De Jure Directors.** De jure directors are those officially appointed and recorded as directors with the
Registrar of Companies at Companies House. A
private company is legally required to have a minimum of one de jure director, while public companies must appoint at least two. These directors have
undergone formal processes to be legally recognised
in their positions.

A classic example is the CEO of a large corporation who has
been officially appointed and registered as a director. They
attend board meetings, make strategic decisions, and are
publicly recognised as a key figure in the company.

(b) **De Facto Directors.** De facto directors, though
lacking formal appointment or registration, effectively perform the duties of a director. They are recognised within the company and externally as fulfilling the director role despite needing to be offi-

cially appointed. They bear the same legal obligations as de jure directors due to their influential role in managing the company.

> Consider a senior manager who, despite not being officially appointed as a director, routinely makes crucial decisions and is involved in the strategic planning of the company. Employees and external parties often perceive this manager as having the authority of a director.

(c) **Shadow Directors.** Shadow directors are individuals who, without a formal appointment, exert substantial influence on the board's decision-making. These individuals guide the actions of the officially appointed directors. The Companies Act 2006 regards shadow directors on equal footing with de facto or de jure directors in terms of legal responsibilities, except for professional advisors who are explicitly excluded from being classified as shadow directors.

> An influential investor who isn't officially a director but whose suggestions and directives are routinely followed by the board could be seen as a shadow director. This investor might not attend board meetings but has significant behind-the-scenes influence.

(d) **Executive and Non-Executive Directors.** A balanced board generally consists of both executive and non-executive directors. Executive directors are engaged in the daily management. They are company employees, whereas non-executive directors typically assume advisory roles, focusing on oversight and supervision without direct involvement in daily management tasks.

Executive Director: The Chief Financial Officer (CFO) of a company, handling day-to-day financial operations, is an executive director.

Non-Executive Director: A retired industry expert serving on the board, providing oversight and advice without being involved in everyday company operations.

(e) **Alternate Directors.** These are individuals appointed by an existing director to attend and vote in board meetings in their absence, ensuring continued representation and decision-making.

A scenario could involve a director who is unable to attend a crucial board meeting due to a scheduling conflict, so they appoint a trusted senior manager to attend and vote on their behalf.

(f) **Nominee Directors.** A nominee director represents the interests of a specific stakeholder, usually a shareholder. They are considered de jure directors and must prioritise the company's overall interests while representing a particular party.

A venture capital firm invests in a startup and, as part of the investment agreement, appoints one of its partners as a director on the startup's board to represent its interests and investment.

1.3 Authority of Directors

Directors are the primary individuals responsible for managing a company, as opposed to the shareholders. This is particularly common in private limited companies where the members often double as directors. The extent of a director's powers is outlined in the company's articles of association.

According to the model articles:

(a) **Scope of Directors' Powers**: The model articles typically grant directors comprehensive authority to manage the company, allowing them to exercise all the powers of the company. This authority is subject only to specific limitations or provisions in the articles.

Imagine "Tech Innovations Ltd", a private limited company specialising in software development. The company's articles grant its board of directors the power to make most decisions, including entering into significant contracts, hiring key staff, and setting business strategies.

For instance, the directors decide to expand the business into a new European market. This decision involves assessing risks, allocating resources, and developing a market entry strategy.

All these actions fall within the directors' powers as granted by the company's articles.

(b) **Shareholder Oversight:** While directors have broad powers, shareholders maintain a degree of oversight. The model articles often include provisions that allow shareholders to influence directors' decisions. Shareholders can pass a special resolution requiring a 75% majority vote to direct the directors to undertake or refrain from specific actions.

The shareholders of "Tech Innovations Ltd" are concerned about a new venture into high-risk markets and believe it could endanger the company's financial stability. They convene a general meeting and pass a special resolution with a 75% majority vote, directing the directors not to proceed with the expansion.

This resolution is binding on the directors, illustrating the shareholders' ability to influence major strategic decisions despite the directors' broad powers.

Board-Level Decision Making:

(a) **Collective Exercise of Powers:** Directors are expected to collaborate as a board in exercising their powers. This collective decision-making ensures a balanced approach to managing the company's affairs.

The board of "Tech Innovations Ltd" decides to delegate the task of developing a new software product to a specialised committee. This committee comprises a few directors and senior managers with relevant expertise. The board sets the committee's objectives, budgets, and timelines but leaves the operational details to the committee. This delegation showcases the board's ability to assign specific tasks while retaining control and responsibility.

(b) **Delegation of Authority:** The board of directors can delegate their powers to individuals or committees as deemed appropriate. This delegation can be for various purposes, such as managing specific aspects of the business or for operational efficiency.

The directors of "Tech Innovations Ltd" appoint one of their number, Jane, as the Managing Director. They delegate day-to-day operational powers to her, allowing her to make decisions on routine matters without needing the entire board's approval.

This delegation streamlines decision-making for everyday business operations while the board focuses on broader strategic issues.

1.4 The Decision-Making Dynamics in a Company

In the corporate hierarchy, directors are usually at the helm of day-to-day management, making crucial operational decisions. Yet, as company owners, the overarching authority of shareholders becomes particularly relevant for decisions that might significantly reshape the company's structure or where directors' personal financial interests are at stake.

(a) **Necessity of Shareholder Approval in Directorial Decisions.** Directorial Decisions with Personal Interests: Directors' decisions that involve their financial interests require explicit approval from shareholders. This protocol ensures that the company's welfare takes precedence over any personal gains of directors.

A situation where the board proposes offering a director an employment contract exceeding two years is a typical instance where shareholder sanction is required.

Such a measure ensures that long-term commitments involving directors align with the company's broader strategic goals.

(b) **Shareholder-Dominant Decisions.** Legislatively and Article-Mandated Decisions: Some decisions, as prescribed by the Companies Act 2006 or the company's articles of association, are solely in the shareholders' domain. These often include pivotal changes to the company's constitution or governance.

Amending the articles of association is a decision that falls squarely with the shareholders. Effecting such a change demands a special resolution passed by a supermajority (75%) of shareholders, affirming that significant alterations to the company's foundational structure have robust backing from its owners.

1.5 Directors as Representatives of the Company

Directors operate as the company's agents, similar to partners in a partnership, with the authority to engage the company in legal agreements and liabilities, both contractually and in tort, as long as they act within their defined powers.

(a) **Apparent Authority:** This concept refers to a situation where a third party reasonably believes that a director is authorised to act on its behalf based on the company's conduct or representations. This belief can be formed simply by the director's role in the company unless evidence suggests the director lacks such authority.

(b) **Explicit Authority.** A director's explicit authority is outlined either in the company's articles or through board resolutions. These documents specify the extent and limits of a director's powers. Typically, board decisions are collective, but specific duties or powers might be assigned to individual directors or committees.

(c) **Perceived Authority.** Although directors usually require board consensus to bind the company, there are scenarios where a director's past interactions or the company's conduct could create a perception of individual authority.

(c) Formalising Agreements and Documents:

- **Contractual Engagements:** Companies can form contracts using their corporate seal or through a representative with the proper authority.

- **Document Execution Procedures:** Official documents can be legally executed by affixing the corporate seal or through the signatures of two directors, one director and the company secretary, or a single director in the presence of a witness.

1.6 Directorial Duties and Obligations

(a) **Core Fiduciary Responsibilities.** Directors must prioritise the company's interests, focusing on integrity and good faith.

A director of "GreenTech Ltd" rejects a lucrative contract with a supplier known for environmental malpractices, prioritising the company's commitment to sustainability over short-term profits.

(b) **Extended Responsibility Post-Directorship.** Directors' duties may continue to apply after their tenure, particularly regarding information and opportunities accessed during their service.

After leaving "FinanceCorp Inc.," a former director doesn't use the insider financial information obtained during their tenure for personal investment or advising another company.

(c) **Adherence to Given Authority:** Directors must operate within the bounds of their designated powers per the company's constitution.

A "BuildIt Construction" director refrains from making unilateral decisions on significant investments, adhering to the board's collective decision-making process outlined in the company's constitution.

(d) **Obligation to Foster Company Success.** Considering various broader factors, directors need to act in a manner they believe will best promote the company's success.

The "HealthFoods Ltd" directors decide to invest in employee wellness programs, believing this will enhance long-term productivity and company reputation.

(e) **Standard of Competence and Diligence.** Directors are expected to demonstrate care, skill, and diligence aligning with a general standard and capabilities.

A director with extensive tech experience at "InnovateNow Ltd" diligently uses their expertise to guide the company's technological strategy and advancements.

(f) **Mandate for Independent Decision-Making.** Directors must make decisions independently, without undue influence, while aligning with the company's agreements or constitution.

An "EduWorld Schools" director seeks expert advice on new educational technologies but ensures the final decision aligns with the company's educational goals and values.

(g) **Requirement to Evade Interest Conflicts.** Directors should avoid situations where their personal interests conflict or might conflict with the company's.

A director of "AutoWorks Ltd," who also owns a car parts supply business, recuses themselves from board decisions involving supplier contracts to avoid conflict of interest.

(h) **Prohibition on Accepting External Advantages.** Directors are barred from accepting benefits from third parties related to their directorial role, except where such benefits don't pose a conflict of interest risk.

A director of "FashionTrends Co." declines a luxury holiday gift from a fabric supplier to avoid any perception of influence on supplier selection.

(i) **Disclosure of Personal Interests.** Directors must disclose any direct or indirect personal interest in company transactions.

A director at "MediaMogul Enterprises" discloses their minor stake in a competing media company during board discussions about potential mergers.

(j) **Restrictions on Directorial Financial Arrangements.** Any financial arrangements, like loans or guarantees between directors and the company, require the approval of its members.

"TechGiant Inc." seeks and obtains shareholder approval before providing a loan to one of its directors for a significant
investment related to company business.

1.7 Framework for Board Meeting Opera-
tions

(a) **Procedure for Summoning a Meeting.** Initiating a board meeting involves a director notifying
others or instructing the company secretary to issue
a notice. The requirement for 'reasonable notice' is
adaptable to the situation's urgency and proximity
of the directors.

(b) **Mechanics of Decision-Making.** The process
for making decisions in a board meeting typically
involves a majority vote. In tie situations, the chair-
person may have a deciding vote. Directors with
conflicts of interest are generally excluded from voting and the quorum calculation.

(c) **Quorum Establishment Criteria.** The minimum number of directors required to validate a meeting, or the quorum, is usually set at two or more.
This number might be affected if a director has a
personal stake in the matter discussed.

(d) **Alternative Resolution Adoption.** Directors can
pass resolutions without a physical meeting, requir-

ing unanimous consent from all directors as opposed
to the majority rule applicable in regular meetings.

1.8 Directors' Entitlements to Remuneration and Reimbursements

The Companies Act 2006 acknowledges the likelihood of
directors having service contracts, with their entitlements
typically outlined in these agreements. When a director's
service contract is under consideration by the board, they
are excluded from the quorum and voting process related
to their contract.

(a) **Determining Director Compensation:** Under
the model articles for private companies limited by
shares, it is within the board's discretion to decide
what constitutes fair compensation for the directors.
This arrangement allows flexibility in determining
remuneration based on company performance, the
director's role, and market standards.

(b) **Reimbursement of Expenses:** The model articles also permit the company to reimburse directors
for reasonable expenses incurred while attending
meetings or conducting company business. This ensures that directors are financially supported while
performing their duties for the company.

These provisions in the Companies Act 2006 and the model articles reflect the understanding that directors, as key figures in the company's governance, should be appropriately compensated and not bear out-of-pocket expenses for their service to the company.

1.9 Director Termination and Legal Restrictions

(a) **Shareholder Authority to Remove Directors.** The Companies Act 2006 empowers shareholders to remove a director through a simple majority vote. Notably, this decision must be made with a written resolution:

- **Limited Override Possibilities:** Although the shareholders' right to remove a director typically supersedes conflicting articles or service contract provisions, a Bushell v Faith clause might restrict this power by giving extra voting weight to a director who is also a shareholder.

- **Contractual Implications:** Dismissing a director might necessitate compensation for the loss of office and damages for breaching the service contract.

- **Procedure for Removal Proposal:** Proposing a director's removal requires at least 28 days' notice before a general meeting. The director must be informed and entitled to submit a written statement to the shareholders and speak at the meeting.

(b) **Rotational Retirement in PLCs.** For PLCs, model articles stipulate that all directors must retire at the first annual meeting, with subsequent yearly meetings requiring the retirement of directors appointed since the last meeting or those not reappointed during the previous two meetings. This allows new shareholders to influence the board's composition.

(c) **Grounds for Disqualification.** Under the Company Directors Disqualification Act 1986, directors can be disqualified for general misconduct or unfitness, prohibiting them from directorship roles, managing company affairs, or acting as a company receiver.

- **Misconduct Criteria:** Disqualification can result from serious offences related to company management, persistent legislative breaches, fraud in winding up, or non-compliance with required filings.

- **Unfitness Standard:** Disqualification for unfitness considers a director's conduct in managing an insolvent company and can result from public interest investigations.

- **Alternative to Court Proceedings:** Directors may opt for a voluntary disqualification undertaking, avoiding court but accepting disqualification.

2. Company Secretary Role and Requirements

Under the Companies Act 2006, while private companies are not obligated to appoint a company secretary, public companies must ensure they have a qualified individual in this role. The company's directors are usually responsible for appointing and dismissing the company secretary.

2.1 Eligibility Criteria for Company Secretaries

For a public company, the secretary must meet specific qualifications to ensure they can perform their duties competently. These qualifications include:

(a) **Previous experience** in a similar role at a public company.

(b) **Membership in recognised professional bodies** related to accountancy or secretarial work.

(c) **Legal qualifications** as a barrister, advocate, or solicitor in the UK.

(d) **Other professional experiences or affiliations** that the directors deem adequate for the role.

2.2 Responsibilities and Authority of Company Secretaries

Though not legislated, the company secretary's role typically involves critical administrative tasks. Their duties often encompass managing company records, documenting proceedings of meetings, and ensuring the company meets its statutory obligations.

(a) **Delegated and Implied Powers:** While the secretary's powers are often explicitly defined by the board, they may also carry implied or apparent authority, particularly in administrative matters.

3. Auditor Appointment in Companies

The Companies Act mandates that all companies must maintain proper accounts, with larger companies required to have these accounts audited by a qualified auditor.

The criteria for determining whether a company is large enough to require an auditor include annual turnover and employee numbers. Directors are responsible for appointing auditors in companies where auditing is a statutory requirement.

CHAPTER 6. OVERVIEW OF COMPANY MEMBERSHIP

1. Shareholders and their status

As critical company members, shareholders acquire their status in various ways: by being among the initial subscribers during the company's formation, purchasing newly issued shares, or transferring existing shares.

Their principal role revolves around providing financial support to the company. Official membership for a person is established at the point of the company's registration or when their information is added to the company's register of members.

A shareholder may also be categorised as a Person with Significant Control (PSC) if they meet specific criteria, which include:

(a)   Holding **more than 25%** of the company's shares, directly or indirectly.

(b)   Possessing **over 25%** of the voting rights in the company, either directly or indirectly.

(c) Having **the authority to appoint** or remove the majority of the board of directors, directly or indirectly.

(d) Exercising, or having the potential to exercise, significant influence or control over the company.

When a shareholder is designated as a PSC, it is mandatory to record detailed information about them in the company's PSC register. This requirement is a part of the broader regulatory measures to ensure transparency and clarity in companies' governance and control mechanisms.

2. Shareholder Rights and Influence

As a company member, a shareholder is endowed with specific rights concerning the company. These primarily include the entitlement to receive dividends and the right to vote on various company decisions (resolutions).

Despite the directors managing the company's daily operations, shareholders influence certain critical company decisions significantly. This influence is granted through legislation and the company's articles, ensuring that shareholders play a crucial role in shaping the company's strategic direction and governance.

3. Dividend Declaration Process

The decision to propose a dividend lies primarily with the directors. They evaluate the company's financial statements and assess if sufficient profits are available for distributing dividends.

Once the directors decide to recommend a dividend, the shareholders turn to either approve, modify or reject this recommendation through an ordinary resolution. Shareholders have the flexibility to reduce the dividend amount but cannot exceed the figure proposed by the directors.

3.1 Consequences of Distributing Unlawful Dividends

Dividends distributed in a manner that violates legal stipulations, particularly those not sourced from available profits, are deemed unlawful. Shareholders who are aware, or should reasonably be aware, that a dividend is unlawfully declared are obligated to repay it.

Additionally, directors may face personal liability for the unlawful declaration of dividends, as they are responsible for initially recommending the dividend distribution to the shareholders. This liability underscores the importance of thorough and prudent financial assessments by directors before proposing dividends.

4. Shareholder Resolutions and Voting Rights

Shareholder resolutions, crucial decisions impacting the company, are passed during company meetings, with detailed procedures outlined in the chapter on joint decision-making.

The nature of the voting rights available to shareholders is primarily determined **by the type of shares they hold.**

(a) **Ordinary Shareholders:** Typically, ordinary shareholders possess full voting rights. This means they can vote on a wide range of resolutions that affect the company, encompassing significant decisions about its operation, management, and strategic direction.

(b) **Preference Shareholders:** In contrast, preference shareholders usually have limited voting rights, primarily focused on matters that directly impact their specific class rights. These include resolutions that pertain solely to the rights or interests of the preference shareholders, such as changes to dividend policies or modifications to the rights attached to the preference shares.

5. Process and Implications of Shareholder Derivative Actions

Shareholder derivative claims are legal mechanisms that allow shareholders to take action against directors or other relevant individuals on behalf of the company, particularly in cases where the company's board is unlikely to address alleged breaches of duty.

(a) **Who Can File Claims:** Such claims can be initiated by current shareholders or those who have inherited shares. The scope of defendants includes directors, shadow directors, and others who may have breached their duties to the company.

(b) **Claims from Past Events:** Shareholders are entitled to file claims for breaches that occurred before they acquired shares in the company.

(c) **Judicial Scrutiny Process:** The court's examination of a derivative claim involves **two stages:**

   • **Preliminary Assessment:** The court first determines whether a prima facie case is based on the submitted application and evidence. Absence of such a case results in the dismissal of the claim.

- **In-depth Analysis:** If a prima facie case exists, the court evaluates further to decide whether a person acting in the company's best interest would pursue the claim. It also considers if the action was, or would likely be, authorised by the company. Additionally, the court assesses the shareholder's intentions, the action's relevance to the company's success, and whether the shareholder has alternative personal remedies.

(d) **Outcomes of Successful Claims:** Any damages awarded from these claims are for the company. While the Companies Act 2006 doesn't explicitly state common law suggests that the company may be obliged to cover the legal expenses of the shareholder who initiated the claim, maintaining the principle of justice and fairness in holding directors accountable.

6. Safeguarding Minority Shareholder Interests

When directors do not take appropriate action, the decision to initiate a claim on behalf of the company or to ratify the directors' actions usually rests with the majority shareholders. Minority shareholders typically lack the power to instigate such actions.

However, common law acknowledges specific exceptions to protect the interests of minority shareholders.

If minority shareholders believe that the company's affairs are being conducted in a way that is unfairly prejudicial to their interests, they have the right to seek legal recourse. Unfair prejudice might include being excluded from management in a quasi-partnership, improper use of directorial powers, excessive remuneration to directors, or the nonpayment of dividends. In such cases, the court can intervene, and a common remedy is to order the purchase of the aggrieved shareholder's shares.

Additionally, regardless of their shareholding size, any shareholder can apply to have the company wound up if it is solvent and if they can demonstrate that it is just and equitable. However, winding up the company is generally considered a last resort due to its finality and the potential for shareholders to receive less than the value of their shares.

More often, if a minority shareholder has lost confidence in the board of directors, negotiating a sale of their shares is a preferable alternative, as it allows for resolving disputes without dissolving the company.

7. Shareholder Access to Company Records

Shareholders have specific rights to examine essential documents within the company, reinforcing the principles of transparency and accountability in corporate management.

(a) **Director Service Contracts Review:** Shareholders can inspect the service contracts of the company's directors. These documents must be kept at the company's registered office and accessible for at least one year after a director's departure.

(b) **Register of Members Inspection:** Shareholders also have the right to view the register of members. This register, usually maintained at the registered office, **should contain:**

- Names and addresses of all members.

- Registration and cessation dates of membership.

- Details of members' shareholdings.

- An index of members for companies with more than 50 members.

(c) **Request Protocol for Inspection:** Shareholders wishing to inspect these records must submit a formal request, including their details, the inspection's purpose, and any third-party information-sharing intentions.

(d) **Company's Response Duty:** The company must facilitate the inspection within five working days unless it petitions the court for denial based on the request's inappropriate nature. Inappropriate purposes include personal and commercial benefits rather than legitimate shareholder interests.

CHAPTER 7. JOINT DECISION-MAKING IN COMPANIES

1. Conducting Shareholder Meetings

The requirement for holding shareholder meetings varies depending on the type of company:

(a) **Public Companies:** Public companies must conduct an Annual General Meeting (AGM) annually. This statutory requirement ensures regular shareholder involvement in significant company matters.

(b) **Private Companies:** In contrast, private companies are not legally obligated to hold AGMs, although they may choose to do so.

Both private and public companies can convene general shareholder meetings as needed. These meetings are platforms for making pivotal decisions, such as appointing directors and voting on various resolutions brought forward by the board or shareholders under specific conditions (detailed in subsequent sections).

The structure of these meetings is designed to facilitate shareholder participation in the strategic direction and oversight of the company, complementing the day-to-day management by the board of directors.

1.1 Procedures for Convening Shareholder Meetings

As per statutory guidelines, organising shareholder meetings in a company is primarily the responsibility of the directors.

However, there are certain circumstances where others have the authority to call for a meeting:

(a) **Shareholder-Initiated Meetings:** Shareholders holding at least 5% of the company's paid-up voting share capital can compel the directors to arrange a meeting. Directors must schedule the meeting within 21 days of the request, which should occur within 28 days. If directors do not fulfil this obligation, the shareholders who made the request, or any shareholders representing a majority of the voting rights, may organise the meeting themselves and are eligible for reimbursement from the company for related expenses.

(b) **Auditor-Requested Meetings:** An auditor who resigns can ask the directors to call a meeting. This is mainly to provide an avenue for the auditor to discuss the reasons for their resignation.

(c) **Court-Mandated Meetings:** In exceptional cases, such as shareholder deadlock preventing the company from organising a meeting, a court can step in and order that a meeting be held.

These rules ensure a balanced approach in a company's governance, allowing directors, shareholders, auditors, and even the court to initiate shareholder meetings when necessary, thus safeguarding the interests of all major parties involved.

1.2 Notification Requirements for Shareholder Meetings

Effective communication and adequate notice are crucial for conducting shareholder meetings in a company. Specific guidelines govern the process of notifying relevant parties about these meetings:

(a) **Recipients of the Notice:** Notice must be sent to all shareholders, directors, personal representatives of deceased shareholders, trustees in bankruptcy of bankrupt shareholders, and the company's auditor if appointed. Notices can be distributed through various means, including written or electronic forms like email or website notifications.

(b) **Details Included in the Notice:** The notice should clearly state the company's name, the time, date, and location of the meeting, an outline of the agenda, information about proxy appointment rights, and the complete text of any special resolutions to be discussed.

(c) **Timing for the Notice:** A minimum of 14 clear days' notice is required for a meeting unless the company's articles stipulate a more extended period. 'Clear days' excludes the day the notice is sent and the meeting day. For non-hand-delivered notices, an additional 48 hours should be added for the notice to be considered served.

(d) **Consequences of Inadequate Notice:** Insufficient notice may lead to disputes from shareholders who are dissatisfied with decisions made at the meeting, potentially resulting in those actions being challenged or invalidated.

(e) **Provision for Short Notice:** Meetings can be convened on shorter notice if consented to by a majority representing at least 90% of the shares (or 95% in non-traded public companies). However, short notice cannot override specific requirements like having documents at the registered office 15 days before the meeting.

1.3 Minimum Attendance for Valid Shareholder Meetings

A quorum is essential for a shareholders' meeting to conduct valid decision-making. A quorum refers to the minimum number of members required to be present for the proceedings to be legitimate.

The standard quorum for a shareholder meeting, unless specified differently in the company's articles, is two members. This rule holds unless the company has only a single member. In such cases, proxies can also contribute to the quorum count.

However, a situation where one shareholder attends the meeting and simultaneously acts as a proxy for another does not suffice to establish a quorum.

1.4 Voting on Shareholder Resolutions

In shareholder meetings, resolutions are passed based on shareholder votes and categorised into ordinary and extraordinary resolutions.

(a) **Ordinary Resolutions:** To pass an ordinary resolution, a simple majority vote – over 50% – of the members present at the meeting is required. These resolutions typically cover standard or routine decisions within the company's operations.

(b) **Special Resolutions:** A higher threshold is required for a special resolution to be approved – the affirmative vote of at least 75% of the members present. Special resolutions are usually reserved for more significant company actions that could adversely affect shareholders. The Companies Act 2006 mandates special resolutions for critical decisions such as amendments to the company's articles of association, reducing the company's share capital, initiating the winding up of the company, and changing the company's name. Additionally, the company's articles might specify other matters that require a special resolution. It's important to note that all special resolutions must be registered at Companies House within 15 days of their approval.

1.5 Voting Procedures in Company Meetings

Voting at company meetings typically follows a standard procedure, but alternative methods can be invoked **under certain conditions:**

(a) **Show of Hands:** The default voting method in company meetings is a show of hands. Each shareholder, whether attending personally or represented by a proxy, is entitled to one vote. This approach emphasises equality among shareholders regardless of the number of shares owned.

(b) **Poll Voting:** An alternative to the show of hands is poll voting, in which anyone can request the following:

- **At least five shareholders** were present at the meeting.

- Shareholders represent **more than 10% of the total voting rights.**

- Shareholders holding **more than 10% of the company's issued share capital.**

(c) In a poll vote, **the voting power shifts from one vote per shareholder to one vote per share held.** This method can significantly alter the voting outcome, particularly when shareholding is unevenly distributed, as it gives greater weight to those holding more shares.

These voting methods ensure that while the default approach treats all shareholders equally, there is an option to reflect the proportionate influence of shareholders based on their shareholding. This flexibility allows for a fair representation of interests in critical company decisions.

ABC Ltd. is holding an annual general meeting (AGM) to decide on a significant company policy change. The company has 100 shareholders, and the policy change requires a majority vote to pass.

Show of Hands Voting:

In the meeting, a vote is initially called using the show of hands method. Each of the 40 shareholders present at the meeting, including those representing other shareholders through a proxy, raises a hand to cast their vote. In this scenario, each person's vote is equal, regardless of how many shares they own. Suppose 25 vote in favour and 15 against; the resolution would pass based on the majority of hands raised.

Poll Voting:

However, a group of shareholders who own a significant portion of the company's shares request a poll vote instead. In this case, the voting power is based on the number of shares each shareholder owns. Let's say ABC Ltd. has 1,000 shares in total. If a shareholder who opposed the policy change owns 300 shares, they now have 300 votes in the poll, giving them more influence than the single vote they had in the show of hands method. The outcome of the vote could be significantly different under a poll, especially if large shareholders have differing views from the majority of smaller shareholders.

In this example, the voting method can drastically affect the decision-making process in the company, highlighting the importance of understanding and choosing the appropriate voting method in company meetings.

1.6 Process for Passing Resolutions via Written Agreement in Private Companies

Private companies can pass resolutions through a written agreement instead of holding a traditional shareholder meeting. This method is particularly advantageous for smaller companies due to its efficiency and cost-effectiveness.

(a) **Scope of Written Resolutions:** Written resolutions can be employed for ordinary and extraordinary resolutions, adhering to the exact majority requirements as if the resolution were passed at a meeting. However, this method cannot remove a director or an auditor.

(b) **Initiation of Written Resolutions:** The board of directors typically proposes a written resolution. Nonetheless, shareholders holding a minimum of 5% of the company's total voting rights can compel the directors to circulate a written resolution.

(c) **Distribution of Resolution Documents:** The proposed written resolution must be sent to all voting-eligible members. It should include clear instructions on how shareholders can indicate their agreement and the expiry date of the resolution, usually set at 28 days from the date of circulation unless the company's articles specify a different duration.

(d) **Accompanying Documentation:** Any documents available at a general shareholders' meeting or at the registered office 15 days before such a meeting must also be distributed along with the written resolution.

(e) **Voting Thresholds and Basis:** The voting thresholds for passing a written resolution align with those in general meetings—over 50% for ordinary resolutions and 75% or more for special resolutions. However, the critical difference lies in the voting base; written resolutions require the stated percentage of all eligible voting shareholders, not just those who attend a meeting in person or by proxy. Additionally, the voting is based on one vote per share held, contrasting with the one vote per attending shareholder system typically used in meetings.

2. Summary of Joint Decision Making in Companies

A company's management often involves collaborative decision-making between the board of directors and the shareholders. While the directors handle routine operational decisions, key strategic actions require shareholder consent, particularly those impacting shareholders or involving directors' conflicting interests.

2.1 Decisions Exclusively by Directors

The board follows a straightforward process for decisions that fall solely under the directors' purview, such as changing the company's registered office address. They pass the necessary resolution and handle any associated administrative or filing requirements without shareholder involvement.

2.2 Decisions Needing Both Directors and Shareholder Approval

When a decision necessitates directorial and shareholder approval (like altering the company's name), the process begins with the board's resolution, followed by either convening a shareholder meeting or circulating a written resolution for shareholder approval. Post shareholder approval, the directors may need to meet again for administrative formalities, especially for decisions involving significant company actions.

2.3 Resolutions Requiring Ordinary Shareholder Approval

Certain matters necessitate an ordinary resolution by shareholders unless stated otherwise in the articles. These include:

(a) **Appointing** or removing auditors and directors.

(b) **Approving** annual accounts and reports.

(c) **Declaring** dividends.

(d) **Authorising** shared allotments.

(e) **Approving** substantial property transactions involving directors.

(f) **Ratifying** directors' duty breaches.

(g) **Entering** long-term service contracts with directors.

(h) **Providing** loans to directors.

(i) **Offering** payments for directors' loss of office.

(j) **Initiating** voluntary company winding-up.

2.4 Resolutions Necessitating Special Shareholder Approval

Actions requiring a special resolution include:

(a) **Share buybacks.**

(b) **Modifications** to the company's articles of association.

(c) **Company name changes.**

3. Compliance with Filing Obligations

Whenever a resolution (by the board, shareholders, or both) alters information recorded at Companies House, it's essential to file a record of these changes within 14 days of their approval. This ensures regulatory compliance and keeps the company's public records up-to-date.

CHAPTER 8. COMPAN-IES AND FINANCE STRATEGIES

1. Financing Approaches for Companies

Companies rely on various financing methods, including equity and debt, to fund their initial setup and expansion or to navigate financial challenges.

1.1 Understanding Equity Financing

Equity financing is a capital acquisition method where a company raises funds by selling ownership stakes, or shares, to external investors. When investors provide financial resources to the company, they are, in return, allotted shares, effectively becoming members or shareholders of the company.

This approach is commonly utilised in companies limited by shares, where individuals are allocated a specific number of shares, and their ownership percentage in the company is determined by the proportion of shares they hold. Equity financing is a crucial strategy for businesses seeking to expand or invest in new projects without increasing their debt burden.

(a) **Initial Share Allocation.** During company formation, initial investors (subscribers) agree to buy shares, contributing to the company's initial share capital. This capital, representing the nominal value of shares, forms a non-distributable fund, underpinning the company's financial foundation.

(b) **Subsequent Share Issuance.** Post-formation, companies may issue additional shares for extra capital. Directors usually have inherent authority to allot new shares, subject to any restrictions in the company's articles. Shareholder approval via ordinary resolution is often required for additional issuance.

(c) **Share Issuance Process.** Directors decide the quantity and price of new shares. Usually, shares are issued for cash, but property or other assets may also be acceptable. A share premium account records any amount paid above the nominal value.

(d) **Pre-Emptive Rights for Shareholders.** Existing shareholders often have the first right to buy new shares, maintaining their ownership proportion. The company's articles or a special shareholder resolution can modify or waive this right.

(e) **Share Transferability.** Share transfers involve selling or gifting existing shares. While new shares aren't created, the selling shareholder benefits financially, not the company. The company's articles regulate transferability.

1.2 Debt Financing Explained

Debt financing is a capital-raising strategy where a company acquires funds through borrowing. The company forms a creditor-debtor relationship with an external creditor during this process. The company commits to repaying the borrowed amount to the creditor.

Notably, the creditor does not gain any ownership stake in the company in debt financing. This form of financing is distinct from equity financing, where capital is raised for a share of ownership in the company.

(a) **Borrowing Authority.** Directors typically have the authority to decide on borrowing, barring any article-imposed restrictions.

(b) **Loan Types.** Loans can be either secured (with collateral) or unsecured. Secured loans include mortgages and fixed charges on assets. Floating charges cover assets that fluctuate, like inventory. Proper registration of charges is crucial for enforceability.

(c) **Debt Securities.** Debt securities are tradable documents evidencing a loan. They're akin to negotiable IOUs, promising interest and loan repayment.

2. Tax Considerations in Financing

Companies are taxed under the corporation tax system, where companies must pay tax on their profits. This tax regime is distinct from individuals' income tax obligations.

Additionally, shareholders who have invested in a company through share purchases are subject to income tax on any dividends they receive from these investments. It's important to note that the taxation of dividends for shareholders and the corporation tax liabilities of companies are two separate considerations, each governed by its rules and regulations.

This distinction is crucial for understanding the financial responsibilities and implications for companies and their investors. Detailed information on corporation tax for companies and income tax for individuals, particularly concerning dividends, is typically covered in specialised tax law materials.

CHAPTER 9. RECORD-KEEPING, FILING, AND DISCLOSURE IN COMPANIES

Companies benefiting from limited liability status are subject to mandatory transparency regarding specific aspects of their operations and financial status. This requirement ensures that potential investors and other interested parties have access to crucial information, aiding informed decision-making.

While the company's articles of association are accessible at Companies House, other vital details must also be publicly disclosed.

Critical areas of required disclosure include:

(a) **Annual Accounts and Reports:** Companies must file their annual accounts and reports, providing an overview of their financial performance and condition.

(b) **Confirmation Statement:** An annual confirmation statement, updating or confirming the accuracy of information held by Companies House, is necessary.

(c) **Changes in Company Structure:** Any alterations in the company's structure or management, such as changes in directors or shifts in share capital, must be reported.

(d) **Register of Members:** Companies should maintain an up-to-date register of members, which includes shareholder details and shareholdings and is available for public inspection.

(e) **Register of People with Significant Control (PSC):** Details of individuals or entities with significant control over the company, generally those with over 25% shareholding or voting rights, must be recorded and disclosed.

(f) **Registered Office Address:** Companies must disclose their registered office address as the official communications and legal documents address.

(g) **Details of Mortgages and Charges:** Companies must file particulars of any mortgages or charges against the company, providing insight into its financial commitments.

1. Organisational Record-keeping in Companies

The Companies Act 2006 mandates private companies to maintain various registers and records to ensure transparency and accountability. These records are essential for both internal management and regulatory compliance.

Critical aspects of company recordkeeping include:

(a)   **Registers:** Private companies are required to keep and regularly update several registers, **including:**

- **Register of Members:** List all company shareholders, shareholdings, and related details.

- **Register of Directors:** Recording the names and details of all company directors.

- **Register of Secretaries:** Detailing the names and particulars of company secretaries.

- **Register of Charges:** Keeping track of any charges or encumbrances against the company's assets.

- **Register of People with Significant Control (PSC):** Documenting individuals or entities with substantial control or influence over the company.

These registers must be available for inspection at the company's registered office, with some accessible to members for free and others to the public for a fee. Additionally, specific registers can be kept at Companies House.

(b) **Meeting Minutes:** Minutes from all general shareholders' meetings must be preserved for at least ten years. These records must be accessible to shareholders for inspection without charge. They serve as an official record of the decisions and discussions during these meetings.

(c) **Directors' Service Contracts:** Copies of service contracts with directors must be retained for at least one year after the termination of each director's service. These contracts should be available for members to inspect, providing transparency about the terms of directors' engagements with the company.

This systematic recordkeeping is crucial in corporate governance, providing a clear and accessible history of the company's decisions, agreements, and structural changes.

It ensures stakeholders can effectively monitor and review the company's operations and governance practices. Compliance with these recordkeeping requirements is a legal obligation and a best practice for maintaining corporate integrity and stakeholder trust.

2. Mandatory Company Filings at Companies House

The Companies Act 2006 sets out several compulsory filing requirements for companies registered in the UK. These filings, submitted to Companies House, play a pivotal role in maintaining corporate transparency and accountability.

(a) Annual Confirmation Statement (Previously Annual Return):

- **Purpose:** Confirms annually that Companies House holds up-to-date information about the company.

- **Statement of Capital:** Required if there have been changes in the company's share capital since the last confirmation.

- **Filing Period:** Must be filed within 14 days of the end of the review period, which is 12 months post-incorporation for the first statement.

- **Legal Consequence:** Failing to file on time is a criminal offence.

(b)   Charges Against Company's Assets:

- **Requirement:** Charges must be registered at Companies House within 21 days of creation.

- **Purpose:** Ensures public record of any charges or encumbrances against the company's assets.

(c)   Annual Accounts:

- **Filing Deadline:** Nine months after the end of the accounting period for private companies and six months for public companies.

- **Public Access:** Accounts are publicly available on the Companies House website once filed.

- **Director Approval:** Directors must approve the accounts, confirming they provide an accurate and fair view of the company's financial status.

- **Audit Report:** Required for medium and large companies, exempt for small companies.

- **Penalties for Non-compliance:** Late filing incurs penalties, potential criminal sanctions, and possible director disqualification.

(d) **Directors' Report** (For Medium and Large Companies):

- **Contents:** Names of directors, dividend recommendations, and other relevant information.

- **Purpose:** Provides insight into the company's management and decision-making processes.

(e) **Strategic Report** (For Medium and Large Companies):

- **Objective:** Offers a comprehensive view of the company's business development and performance.

- **Function:** Assists members in evaluating the directors' performance regarding their duty to promote the company's success.

3. Company's Duty to Update Records

Companies registered in the UK are legally obligated to keep Companies House informed of significant changes in their structure and governance. This obligation ensures that the public register remains an accurate source of corporate information.

Critical updates that must be reported include:

(a) Changes in Directorship or Officers:

- **What to Update:** Appointment, termination, or any changes in the details of directors or company secretaries.

- **Deadline:** Within 14 days of the change.

- **Procedure:** Update the locally kept register and file the appropriate forms with Companies House.

(b) Share Capital Alterations:

- **Ordinary Resolutions for Share Allotment:** File with Companies House within 15 days of approval.

- **Issuance of New Shares:** Notify Companies House within one month of issuance.

- **Special Resolutions:** Such as share capital reduction, to be filed within 15 days, often with additional documentation like a solvency statement.

(c) Change in Registered Office Address:

- **Effective Date:** The change is recognised only after it has been filed and registered with Companies House.

(d) Other Significant Changes:

- **Articles of Association Amendments:** Any modifications must be filed promptly.

- **Significant Transactions or Agreements:** Depending on the nature of the transaction, specific filings may be required.

Non-compliance with these reporting obligations can lead to legal consequences, including penalties for the company and its directors. Companies must have procedures to monitor these changes and ensure timely reporting to maintain their legal standing and uphold transparency. A detailed chart summarising these filing requirements is often provided in corporate compliance resources to assist companies in adhering to these obligations.

CHAPTER 10. INSOLVENCY

4. Overview

Insolvency represents a financial state where an individual or a business cannot meet debt obligations. The implications and procedures for handling insolvency vary depending on the company's structure.

(a) **Sole Proprietorships and Partnerships:** In these business models, the personal assets of the owners or partners may be at risk since there is no legal distinction between personal and business assets.

(b) **Incorporated Businesses** (Limited Liability Partnerships and Companies): These entities enjoy a separate legal identity, meaning the personal assets of the members or shareholders are generally protected.

(c) **Definition of Insolvency:** Insolvency occurs when a debtor (the entity owing money) cannot pay their debts to creditors (those to whom money is owed). This can be due to a lack of liquid assets or when liabilities exceed the value of assets.

The process of resolving insolvency differs significantly based on the type of business entity. For sole proprietors and partnerships, insolvency may lead to personal bankruptcy. For incorporated entities, various insolvency procedures like administration, liquidation, or company voluntary arrangements are typically pursued. Each process aims to either rehabilitate the business or ensure fair distribution of assets to creditors.

2. Bankruptcy for Sole Propri- etors and Partners

Bankruptcy applies when sole proprietors or partners cannot meet their business debts. They have several choices, ranging from informal discussions with creditors to formal bankruptcy. Creditors also have the power to initiate bankruptcy proceedings under certain conditions.

2.1. Options for Debt Negotiation

When an individual or a partner in a business is over-whelmed by debts exceeding their ability to pay, they may opt to negotiate directly with creditors. The debtor's goal in such negotiations is to either secure a reduction in the total debt owed or arrange an extended repayment peri-od. Creditors might be inclined to accept such proposals if they believe that doing so would result in a higher re-covery than what they might receive if the debtor were to declare bankruptcy.

However, these negotiations and any agreements from them are not legally binding on the creditor. Since the debtor does not provide any additional consideration (a fundamental component of enforceable contracts) in exchange for the creditor's agreement to alter the original terms, the creditor retains the right to revert to demanding full payment by the original terms at any time.

Additionally, reaching an agreement with one creditor does not safeguard the debtor from actions initiated by other creditors. This means that even if a debtor successfully negotiates terms with one creditor, other creditors may still proceed with legal actions or demand full repayment as per the initial agreement.

2.2 Individual Voluntary Arrangements: A Collaborative Debt Resolution

An Individual Voluntary Arrangement (IVA) is a formal agreement between a debtor and their creditors, wherein the creditors agree to accept a lesser amount than what is owed. This structured approach circumvents the enforceability issues typical of informal negotiations. An IVA is a feasible option only when the debtor has sufficient funds or anticipates acquiring enough resources to propose a credible repayment plan to the creditors.

The success of an IVA depends on the debtor's ability to offer a reasonable payment plan acceptable to the creditors. This requires carefully assessing the debtor's financial capacity to ensure the proposed payments are realistic and sustainable over the arrangement term. The primary objective of an IVA is to provide a mutually beneficial solution: the debtor gets a manageable way to clear their debts, and the creditors receive a fair portion of the owed amounts. This balance is critical to successfully negotiating and implementing an Individual Voluntary Arrangement.

2.3 Exploring Bankruptcy: A Legal Pathway for Debt Resolution

Bankruptcy represents a judicial pathway for resolving severe financial distress. It involves a legal process where a debtor's assets are liquidated to repay debts, providing a structured approach to debt relief.

Key Aspects of Bankruptcy:

(a) Bankruptcy Process:

- A third party, known as the trustee in bankruptcy, is appointed to manage the debtor's assets.

- The trustee liquidates the debtor's assets to repay as much debt as possible.

- The process follows a strict legal order, prioritising certain debts over others.

(b) Creditor Actions:

- Upon filing for bankruptcy, creditors are required to halt all pursuits of debt repayment from the debtor.

- This provision offers immediate relief to the debtor from persistent debt collection efforts.

(c) Discharge of Debts:

- Most debts are discharged after one year from the commencement of bankruptcy.

- This discharge represents a significant step towards financial rehabilitation for the debtor.

Implications of Bankruptcy:

(a) **Financial Reorganisation:** Bankruptcy provides a mechanism for reorganising a debtor's finances, potentially enabling a fresh start.

(b) **Legal Framework:** The process is governed by specific legislation, ensuring fairness and order in distributing the debtor's assets.

(c) **Relief and Restrictions:** While offering relief from overwhelming debts, bankruptcy also imposes certain restrictions and responsibilities on the debtor.

In essence, bankruptcy is a legal solution for individuals or entities unable to meet their debt obligations. It offers a way to address financial crises while adhering to a legally mandated asset liquidation and debt repayment process.

2.4 Bankruptcy Procedure: Pathways and Official Appointments

As a legal means to address insolvency, bankruptcy can be initiated through various procedures, each with specific conditions and outcomes.

Methods to Initiate Bankruptcy:

(a) Debtor's Application:

- The debtor can apply for bankruptcy online.

- An adjudicator, appointed by the Secretary of State, reviews the application.

- The bankruptcy order is granted if the adjudicator concludes that the debtor cannot pay their debts.

(b) Creditor's Petition:

- Unsecured creditors, collectively owed at least £5,000, can file a petition for bankruptcy against the debtor in court.

- This action is usually taken when creditors believe the debtor cannot meet their debt obligations.

(c) Supervisor's Petition under an IVA:

- If a debtor has an Individual Voluntary Arrangement (IVA) but breaches its terms, hides assets, or gives preference to certain creditors, the IVA's supervisor can petition for the debtor's bankruptcy.

Appointment of an Official Receiver:

(a) Once **a bankruptcy order is issued**, an official receiver is appointed.

(b) **The official receiver**, a civil servant, assumes the role of trustee in bankruptcy.

(c) **Creditors can nominate their trustee**, but the official receiver retains this role without such an appointment.

Role of the Official Receiver:

(a) **Asset Management:** The official receiver manages the debtor's assets, ensuring proper valuation and liquidation.

(b) **Debt Distribution:** They oversee the distribution of proceeds from asset liquidation to creditors, adhering to legal priority orders.

(c) **Administrative Duties:** The receiver also handles various administrative aspects of the bankruptcy process, ensuring compliance with legal requirements.

This procedure offers a structured approach for debtors facing insolvency, providing a fair and orderly process for asset liquidation and debt repayment under the supervision of an appointed trustee.

2.5 Creditor's Application for Bankruptcy: Establishing insolvency

When a creditor seeks to declare a debtor bankrupt, they must demonstrate the debtor's insolvency. This involves proving the debtor's inability to pay their debts. Several methods exist for a creditor to establish this:

Demonstrating Insolvency:

(a) Statutory Demand for Payment of Liquidated Debt:

- Applicable when the debtor owes a fixed, determined debt of £5,000 or more.

- The creditor issues a statutory demand for payment.

- If the debtor fails to pay within three weeks or does not contest the demand legally within this period, their insolvency is presumed.

(b) Statutory Demand for Future Liability:

- It is relevant when the debtor has a future financial obligation exceeding £5,000.

- The creditor serves a statutory demand for evidence of the debtor's ability to pay when the debt becomes due.

- The debtor's failure to demonstrate a reasonable payment prospect or legally challenge the demand leads to an assumption of insolvency.

(c) Failure to Satisfy a Judgment Debt:

- If the debtor is unable to fulfil a judgment debt above £5,000.

- The creditor attempts enforcement of the judgment (e.g., through bailiffs).

- If enforcement efforts are unsuccessful, it indicates the debtor's insolvency.

Legal Implications:

(a) These methods give creditors a **formal mechanism** to assert a debtor's financial incapacity.

(b) The processes **ensure fairness**, allowing the debtor to respond or contest the claims.

(c) Upon successfully **demonstrating insolvency**, the creditor can initiate bankruptcy proceedings against the debtor.

(d) The legal framework **aims to balance** the interests of creditors seeking repayment and debtors facing financial difficulties.

In summary, these procedures offer structured pathways for creditors to legally establish the insolvency of debtors legally, thereby enabling the initiation of bankruptcy proceedings under the defined criteria.

2.6 Bankruptcy Estate: Overview and Process

When an individual is declared bankrupt, their assets form part of what is known as the 'bankruptcy estate'. This estate is managed by a trustee in bankruptcy and is central to the bankruptcy process.

Formation and Management of the Bankruptcy Estate:

(a) Automatic Vesting of Assets:

- Upon declaration of bankruptcy, the debtor's assets automatically become part of the bankruptcy estate.

- This process does not require any legal formalities or documentation from the bankrupt individual (such as stock transfer forms).

(b) Role of the Trustee in Bankruptcy:

- A trustee appointed during the bankruptcy proceedings is responsible for managing the bankruptcy estate.

- The trustee's duties include collecting, valuing, and selling the bankrupt's assets.

(c) Asset Liquidation:

- The trustee liquidates the assets in the bankruptcy estate, converting them into cash.

- This involves selling properties, shares, and other valuable items the bankrupt individual owns.

(d) Repayment of Creditors:

- The funds raised from the liquidation are used to pay off the creditors.

- Payments are made according to a legally defined order of priority.

Key Considerations:

(a) The bankruptcy estate **typically includes most of the debtor's assets, but there are exceptions for essential items** necessary for daily living and work.

(b) The process aims to **distribute the bankrupt individual's assets fairly among creditors.**

(c) It also relieves the bankrupt individual from debt burden, allowing for **a fresh financial start after the bankruptcy period.**

In summary, the bankruptcy estate is a legal construct that enables the equitable distribution of a bankrupt individual's assets among their creditors, managed by the appointed trustee in bankruptcy.

2.7 Exemptions in Bankruptcy Estate

Bankruptcy law provides certain exemptions to ensure that individuals undergoing bankruptcy retain essential items for daily living and work. These exemptions are crucial for balancing the need to satisfy creditors with the bankrupt individual's basic needs.

Personal Exemptions:

(a) **Essential Personal Items:** Items necessary for day-to-day living, such as household furniture and personal effects, are typically exempt from the bankruptcy estate. Tools or equipment required for the bankrupt's employment are also usually exempt, ensuring they can continue to work.

(b) **Income Exemptions:** The bankrupt individual is allowed to retain their salary or wages. However, if their income exceeds what is needed for the reasonable needs of their family, a trustee may apply for an income payment order. This order, lasting up to three years, allocates part of the income towards the repayment of debts.

Bankrupt's Home:

(a) **Home Ownership and Trustee Rights:** The bankrupt's interest in their home passes to the trustee. However, legal or equitable interests in the home must be considered by other parties, such as a spouse or children.

(b) **Complexities of Joint Ownership:** If the home is held in joint names or there are other equitable interests (e.g., a partner's or spouse's claim), these need to be considered. The trustee cannot automatically sell a jointly owned home.

(c) **Occupation Rights:** Spouses or partners may have legal rights of occupation. Children under 18 living in the home grant occupation rights to the bankrupt and their partner.

(d) **Court Involvement:** The trustee requires a court order to sell a home with such interests. After one year, creditors' interests may take precedence, leading to possible sale despite other interests.

2.8 Restrictions on Bankrupt Individuals

Bankruptcy laws impose various restrictions on individuals declared bankrupt. These limitations are designed to protect creditors and mitigate the risk of further financial irresponsibility.

Key restrictions include:

(a) Credit Limitations. Bankrupt individuals can only obtain credit within a specified amount if they disclose their bankruptcy status. This measure prevents the accumulation of additional unmanageable debts during the bankruptcy period.

(b) Professional and Business Restrictions:

- **Prohibition on Directorship.** Individuals undergoing bankruptcy cannot serve as directors in companies. This restriction is intended to prevent potential mismanagement or fraudulent activities in corporate governance.

- **Partnership Restrictions.** Bankrupt individuals are barred from acting as partners in partnerships. This rule aims to protect other partners and the financial integrity of the partnership from potential risks associated with bankruptcy.

(c) Trading Restrictions: Trading under a different name without disclosing the bankruptcy status is prohibited. This transparency ensures that all parties involved in business dealings know the bankrupt individual's financial status, reducing the risk of financial misconduct.

2.9 Bankruptcy Debt Distribution Hierarchy

In bankruptcy proceedings, debts are settled in a specific order to ensure a fair and legally compliant process.

The **hierarchy of debt** distribution in bankruptcy is as follows:

(a) **Bankruptcy Costs.** Priority is given to covering the costs associated with managing the bankruptcy. This includes legal fees, administrative expenses, and other costs incurred during bankruptcy.

(b) **Preferential Debts.** These debts are given higher priority and include employee-related payments include unpaid holiday pay and wages from the last four months. Also, certain taxes are owed to HM Revenue and Customs (HMRC), like VAT, PAYE, and National Insurance contributions.

(c) **Ordinary Unsecured Creditors.** These creditors, who do not have security against the debtor's assets, are paid after the preferential debts are settled. They typically include suppliers, utility providers, and credit card companies.

(d) **Postponed Creditors.** Typically, these are personal creditors like a spouse or civil partner. They are the last in line for debt recovery.

If the available assets are insufficient to satisfy all the creditors within a particular category fully, the available funds are distributed equally among those creditors. Each creditor in that category receives a proportionate share of their claim based on the available assets. This equitable approach ensures that no single creditor in a category is favoured over others.

2.10 Conclusion of Bankruptcy

The termination of bankruptcy, commonly known as discharge, marks the end of the legal process of bankruptcy.

Key points regarding the conclusion of bankruptcy are:

(a) **Automatic Discharge.** A bankrupt individual is typically discharged automatically after one year. This assumes adherence to the restrictions and obligations imposed during the bankruptcy period.

(b) **Compliance with Restrictions.** The discharge is contingent on the bankrupt individual abiding by certain legal restrictions. These include limits on borrowing, refraining from directorship in companies, and transparency about their bankruptcy status when engaging in business.

(c) **Absence of Misconduct.** Discharge is granted provided the bankruptcy was not caused by the individual's dishonest, negligent, or reckless behaviour. Bankruptcies resulting from such misconduct might lead to extended restrictions or additional legal consequences.

(d) **Effect of Discharge.** Once discharged, the individual is released from most of the bankruptcy-related debts. This means they are no longer legally obligated to pay these debts.

(e) **Continued Restrictions for Culpable Conduct.** In bankruptcy cases due to culpable behaviour, restrictions can be extended for up to 15 years. This is to protect the public and the integrity of the financial system.

(f) **Implications for Future Financial Conduct.** Post-discharge, individuals can start rebuilding their financial status, although the history of bankruptcy can affect their credit rating and borrowing capabilities in the short to medium term.

Discharge from bankruptcy marks the end of a significant legal and financial journey, offering an opportunity for a fresh start while maintaining specific long-term responsibilities and consequences.

2.11 Culpable Bankruptcy: Consequences for Dishonest or Reckless Behaviour

In cases where bankruptcy is a result of intentional misconduct, the legal system provides measures to address such culpability:

(a) **Definition of Culpable Bankruptcy.** A bankruptcy is deemed guilty due to the debtor's dishonest, negligent, or reckless actions. This includes fraudulent activities, gross mismanagement of finances, or deliberate evasion of financial responsibilities.

(b) **Extended Court Order.** Culpable bankruptcies may be subject to a court-imposed bankruptcy restriction order (BRO). This order can extend for up to 15 years, significantly longer than the standard one-year discharge period.

(c) **Extended Restrictions.** A BRO extends certain restrictions beyond the standard bankruptcy discharge. These may include prohibitions on borrowing above a specific limit, restrictions on business operations, or limitations on acting as a company director.

(d) **Public Protection.** The primary purpose of these extended orders is to safeguard the public and the financial system from individuals whose past behaviour has shown a disregard for financial obligations and laws.

(e) **Legal and Social Implications.** These extended restrictions can have significant social and economic impacts on the individual, including long-term effects on creditworthiness, employment opportunities, and business activities.

(f) **Legal Review and Appeals.** The imposition of a BRO is subject to legal review, and the affected individual may have the opportunity to contest or appeal the order, typically on grounds of fairness or proportionality.

Culpable bankruptcy cases highlight the intersection of financial distress and ethical conduct, where the legal system seeks to balance the rehabilitation of the bankrupt individual with the protection of broader societal interests.

2.12 Bankruptcy Impact on Partnership and LLP Membership

The implications of an individual partner's bankruptcy on a partnership or Limited Liability Partnership (LLP) can vary depending on the partnership agreement's nature and structure.

(a) Partnership at Will:

- **Dissolution Upon Bankruptcy:** In a general partnership at will, the partnership dissolves when a partner becomes bankrupt.

- **Trustee's Role:** The bankrupt partner's share or interest in the partnership is handled by the trustee in bankruptcy (or a liquidator if the insolvent partner represents a company). This trustee oversees the distribution of the bankrupt partner's share to satisfy their creditors.

(b) Partnership Not at Will:

- **Continuation of Partnership:** If the partnership agreement stipulates that the bankruptcy of a partner does not lead to dissolution, the partnership continues without the bankrupt partner.

- **Buyout of Bankrupt Partner's Interest:** The remaining partners will typically buy the bankrupt partner's interest from the bankruptcy trustee or liquidator. This process is usually guided by the terms of the partnership agreement, particularly those concerning the retirement or exit of partners.

(c) Limited Liability Partnership (LLP):

- **Restriction on Participation:** An undischarged bankrupt individual cannot be a member or participate in managing an LLP unless permitted explicitly by the court.
- **Disposition of Membership Interest:** The trustee in bankruptcy is responsible for realising the value of the bankrupt member's interest in the LLP. This often involves selling the interest to the remaining members, consistent with the LLP's partnership agreement.

Key Considerations:

(a) **Legal Compliance:** These processes must adhere to relevant laws and regulations governing partnerships and LLPs.

(b) **Partnership Agreement:** The specific terms of the partnership or LLP agreement play a crucial role in determining the course of action.

(c) **Creditors' Rights:** The primary aim is to ensure that creditors of the bankrupt partner are appropriately compensated.

(d) **Impact on Business Operations:** The exit of a partner due to bankruptcy can have significant operational and financial implications for the partnership or LLP.

Understanding these dynamics is essential for business partners, as an individual's bankruptcy can have far-reaching consequences on the partnership's structure and financial health.

2.13 Insolvency Scenarios: General Partnership and Limited Liability Partnership (LLP)

Insolvency of All Partners in a General Partnership:

When all partners in a general partnership are declared bankrupt, the partnership undergoes a winding-up process.

This process involves **several key steps:**

(a) **Finalising Contracts:** Ensuring all existing contracts are appropriately completed, transferred, or terminated.

(b) **Ceasing Business Operations:** Halting all business activities of the partnership.

(c) **Resolving Legal Disputes:** Settling any outstanding legal issues or disputes involving the partnership.

(d) **Asset Liquidation:** Selling off the partnership's assets to generate funds.

(e) **Debt Collection:** Gathering any outstanding debts owed to the partnership.

(f) **Distribution to Creditors:** Allocating the collected funds to pay off creditors in an order determined by insolvency laws.

This process is undertaken by an official receiver or an appointed insolvency practitioner and follows the standard protocols for bankruptcy cases.

Insolvency of a Limited Liability Partnership (LLP):

When an LLP faces insolvency and is subject to a winding-up order, it is treated similarly to a limited company in the insolvency process.

The **steps** typically include:

(a) **Appointment of an Official Receiver:** An official receiver or an insolvency practitioner is appointed to oversee the winding-up process.

(b) **Company's Affairs Assessment:** A thorough assessment of the LLP's financial situation is conducted.

(c) **Asset Liquidation:** The LLP's assets are liquidated to convert them into cash.

(d) **Debt Repayment:** Debts are repaid to creditors in a specific legal order.

(e) **Distribution of Remaining Funds:** Any remaining funds after settling debts are distributed per the LLP agreement or insolvency laws.

(f) **Completion of Legal Requirements:** Compliance with all legal formalities for winding up an LLP.

The winding-up process for an LLP is governed by specific regulations and procedures, ensuring that creditors' rights are protected and the dissolution is carried out orderly.

3. Corporate Insolvency: Companies and Limited Liability Partnerships (LLPs)

Corporate insolvency encompasses companies and LLPs struggling financially. This branch of law focuses on safeguarding creditor rights, balancing interests among various creditor groups, facilitating corporate recovery when feasible, and overseeing or penalising company directors as needed.

When a company or LLP cannot individually negotiate with creditors for debt reduction or payment extensions, it may need to resort to formal insolvency procedures. These procedures are generally similar for both companies and LLPs.

3.1 Insolvency Options for Companies

For companies facing insolvency, there are several avenues:

(a) **Receivership:** This process is initiated by secured creditors to reclaim debts explicitly owed to them. It involves the appointment of a receiver who manages the company's assets to recover the debt.

(b) **Administration and Company Voluntary Arrangements:** These methods aim to rescue the company from financial collapse. Administration involves appointing an administrator to oversee the company's affairs, develop a plan to pay creditors and attempt to keep the business running. Company Voluntary Arrangements (CVAs) involve an agreement between the company and its creditors to pay off debts over time while continuing operations.

(c) **Liquidation (Winding Up):** This is the process of dissolving the company. The company's assets are liquidated to pay off debts, and any remaining business activities are concluded. After liquidation, the company ceases to exist.

3.2 Fixed Asset Receivership

While not a direct insolvency procedure, fixed asset receivership often leads to insolvency. It involves the following key elements:

(a) **Breach of Loan Agreement:** When a company borrows funds, creditors may secure the loan against the company's fixed assets (like equipment or property). The creditor can appoint a receiver if the company breaches the loan agreement.

(b) **Role of the Receiver:** The receiver takes control of the charged asset and sells it to repay the secured lender. This action is targeted at recovering the debt for that specific lender and not for the benefit of all creditors.

(c) **Impact on the Company:** Once the asset is sold, the receiver's involvement with the company ends. Depending on the situation, this can lead to broader financial distress for the company, potentially triggering other insolvency processes.

In summary, corporate insolvency procedures provide structured pathways for companies and LLPs in financial distress to either recover or orderly wind down, with the ultimate goal of fairly addressing the claims of creditors.

3.3 Administration: A Comprehensive Guide to Corporate Rescue

Administration is a pivotal insolvency procedure, empowering an appointed administrator to effectively manage, reform, or sell a financially struggling company.

This process is geared towards:

(a) **Aiming** to salvage the company as a viable business entity.

(b) **Securing** a more favourable outcome for the company's creditors compared to liquidation.

(c) **Facilitating** the distribution of assets to satisfy the claims of secured creditors.

Distinct from receivership, the administrator must act in all creditors' collective interest.

Initiation of Administration:

(a) **Court-Driven Administration:** Initiated via a formal court proceeding, this route necessitates the court's conviction of the company's financial incapacity and the comparative benefit of administration over liquidation.

(b) **Director-Led Administration:** Directors or the company can instigate administration outside of court by lodging required documents, given there's no existing winding-up petition. Communication with any qualifying floating charge holder, who may consent or choose an alternate administrator, is essential.

The Concept of Qualifying Floating Charge:

(a) **It signifies a comprehensive charge on the company's assets**, authorising the lender to appoint an administrator or administrative receiver following a contract breach, typically defaulting on payments.

Administrator's Role and Powers:

(a) The administrator, mandated to be a licensed insolvency practitioner, **assumes control over the company's assets,** manages its operations, and takes charge of legal matters, including altering the directorial board.

(b) Additionally, the administrator **investigates previous transactions to enhance asset value** for creditors potentially and can legally challenge directors for wrongful or fraudulent trading practices.

(c) The administrator's strategy **requires approval from most creditors by value.**

The Moratorium (Protection and Opportunity):

(a) Administration **triggers a moratorium, barring third-party rights enforcement and halting** other insolvency actions.

(b) This protective measure grants the administrator **vital time to rejuvenate the company** or arrange a beneficial sale.

3.4 Company Voluntary Arrangement: A Rescue Mechanism for Financially Strained Companies

The CVA is akin to an Individual Voluntary Arrangement (IVA) but tailored for corporate entities. It is a negotiated agreement between a company facing short-term liquidity issues and its creditors. In a CVA, creditors typically agree to accept a reduced settlement of their claims under the premise that this approach will yield a higher return than if the company were liquidated.

Steps Involved in the CVA Process:

(a) **Initiation by Company Directors:** The company's directors initiate the CVA procedure. They must draft a proposal detailing the terms of the arrangement for the creditors.

(b) **Nomination of an Insolvency Practitioner:** The directors nominate a professional insolvency practitioner to oversee and administer the CVA.

(c) **Creditor Approval:** The proposal requires the approval of at least 75% (by value) of the unsecured creditors for the CVA to be implemented. This threshold ensures that a substantial majority of creditors support the arrangement.

(d) **Potential Outcomes:**

- Successful Implementation: If the CVA is approved and implemented, the company can continue its operations while repaying creditors under the revised terms.

- Failure and Alternatives: The company may face liquidation or enter into administration if the CVA fails.

(e) **Moratorium for Small Companies:** Similar to an IVA, a CVA can include a moratorium period. This period offers crucial respite from creditor actions and halts other insolvency proceedings, providing the company a window to restructure its finances and operations effectively.

3.5 Voluntary Liquidation: Understanding the Types and Processes

Voluntary liquidation is a process a company initiates to wind up its affairs and dissolve. There are two primary forms of voluntary liquidation: Members' Voluntary Liquidation (MVL) and Creditors' Voluntary Liquidation (CVL).

(a) **Members' Voluntary Liquidation (MVL).** Suitable for solvent companies looking to cease operations, often due to reasons like owners' retirement or strategic business decisions. The members and directors oversee the entire liquidation process. MVL is exclusive to solvent companies solvent companies, meaning they can pay their debts.

(b) **Creditors' Voluntary Liquidation (CVL).** Begins when directors conclude the company is insolvent and unable to meet its debt obligations. Once initiated, creditors take a more active role in liquidation. Typically, CVL is opted for when the company faces insolvency and continuing business operations might lead to further financial liabilities.

Key Differences - MVL vs. CVL:

MVL is for solvent companies with sufficient assets to cover liabilities, whereas CVL is for insolvent companies facing financial difficulties. MVL often aims for an orderly wind-up and asset distribution among members, while CVL focuses on maximising creditor returns from the liquidated assets.

Liquidation Process:

The decision to liquidate voluntarily is taken through a resolution either by members (in MVL) or directors (in CVL). A licensed insolvency practitioner is appointed to oversee the liquidation process, asset disposal, and debt repayment. Assets are liquidated, and proceeds are distributed according to the hierarchy of creditors' claims (in CVL) or among members (in MVL).

Considerations for Choosing Liquidation Type:

(a) **Financial Health Assessment:** The choice between MVL and CVL hinges on the company's solvency status.

(b) **Objective Assessment:** Companies must assess their objectives, whether an orderly cessation (MVL) or addressing insolvency (CVL).

(c) **Stakeholder Interests:** Consideration of the interests of members and creditors is crucial in determining the appropriate form of liquidation.

3.6 Mandatory Liquidation of a Corporation

(a) Initiation of the Process:

- The process begins when a creditor proves the corporation's insolvency.

- The court evaluates the petition, weighing various factors to determine the company's liquidation necessity.

(b) Function of the Liquidator:

- **Collecting** the company's assets and distributing them to creditors.

- **Oversees** the company's dissolution after orderly settlement of its debts.

(c) Distribution Hierarchy for Creditors:

- **Liquidation Costs:** Initial payments cover the liquidation expenses, including remunerations for the liquidator and associated professionals.

- **Priority Debts:** Includes outstanding wages of employees (restricted to a specific period and capped limit) and tax-related liabilities to HMRC.

- **Secured Debts via Floating Charges:** Debts covered by floating charges are following, consid-

ering their chronological precedence and any
ring-fencing rules.

- **General Unsecured Claims:** All unsecured
debts are addressed at this stage.

- **Shareholder Allocation:** Any remaining assets
are distributed among the shareholders.

4. Recovery of Diverted Assets

Companies or individuals under financial strain may attempt to safeguard assets from legal processes like liquidation, administration, or bankruptcy. This creates a risk where assets are transferred to protect them from creditors or insolvency practitioners.

Liquidators, administrators, or trustees in bankruptcy must act in the best interests of creditors. These practitioners possess the authority to scrutinise pre-insolvency transactions and activities. The insolvency practitioner can request judicial intervention to reverse illegal or improper asset transfers.

Specific Transactions Subject to Reversal:

(a) **Recent Transactions:** Certain asset transfers made shortly before the onset of insolvency may be scrutinised.

(b) **Undervalued Deals:** Transactions where the insolvent entity sold assets for significantly less than their market value.

(c) **Preferential Transfers:** Instances where the insolvent entity favoured specific creditors over others.

(d) **Fraudulent Transactions:** Any asset transfers made to defraud creditors.

4.1 Addressing Preferential Transactions

Preferential Transactions occurs when a debtor conducts a transaction that improves the position of a particular creditor, surety, or guarantor over others in anticipation of insolvency.

Criteria for Establishing a Preference:

(a) **Intentionality Requirement:** The debtor must have deliberately intended to favour the creditor. This intent is presumed if the beneficiary is connected (e.g., a director, family member, or close associate).

(b) **Timing Parameter:** The transaction must have occurred six months before insolvency proceedings (extended to two years for connected persons).

(c) Relevant Dates for Insolvency Onset:

- **Company Liquidation:** Date of the liquidation petition's presentation.

- **Voluntary Liquidation (CVL)**: Date of entering liquidation.

- **Administration:** Earliest of either filing for administration or actual administration onset.

- **Individual Bankruptcy:** Date of the bankruptcy petition presentation.

(d) Legal Implications and Remedies:

- **Voidability:** Such transactions are subject to being declared void at the court's discretion.

- **Court's Orders:** The court may mandate the return of transferred property, refund of sale proceeds, or nullify any created security.

4.2 Addressing Transactions at an Undervalue

Transactions at an Undervalue occur when assets are transferred as a gift or sold for considerably less than their market value, diminishing the value of an insolvent estate.

Timeframe for Review:

(a) **For Companies:** Transactions within two years before insolvency.

(b) **For Individuals:** Transactions within five years before bankruptcy.

Legal Implications and Remedies:

(a) **Consequences:** Similar to preferential transactions, these actions are scrutinised and can be reversed.

(b) **Court's Authority:** The court can order the reversal of the transaction, restoration of assets, or compensation equivalent to the lost value.

Imagine a company, XYZ Ltd, facing financial difficulties and is on the brink of insolvency. Six months before declaring bankruptcy, the company sells valuable machinery to one of the director's relatives at a significantly reduced price. The market value of this machinery is £100,000, but it's sold for just £10,000. This transaction is not in the company's usual course of business and is done solely to transfer the asset out of the company's reach.

Upon entering insolvency proceedings, the practitioner investigates the company's recent transactions and discovers this sale. They determine that it constitutes a transaction at an undervalue, as the machinery was sold for much less than its market value shortly before the insolvency.

This action deprived the insolvency estate of a significant asset that could have been used to repay creditors.

The insolvency practitioner takes the matter to court, and the court agrees that this was a transaction at an undervalue. The court orders that the machinery be returned to XYZ Ltd's insolvency estate or that the relative pays the difference between the sale price and the market value, ensuring that the creditors are not unfairly deprived of potential repayment from the company's assets.

4.3 Insolvency Law: Addressing Transactions at Undervalue

(a) Insolvency Preconditions:

- **For Companies:** A transaction is challengeable if the company was either insolvent at the time or became insolvent due to the transaction. Transactions with a connected person (like a director or their family) inherently assume insolvency.

- **For Individuals:** When a transaction occurs within two years before the bankruptcy petition, proving insolvency is optional. However, insolvency is presumed if the transaction favoured a close relative or business associate.

(b) Defence Mechanism for Companies:

- **Validity Criteria:** A company can defend a transaction if it was conducted genuinely for business purposes, in good faith, and with a belief that it would benefit the company.

(c) Granting Security vs. Undervalue Transactions:

- **Distinction:** Granting security interests in assets, such as liens or mortgages, is not deemed a transaction at undervalue, as it doesn't diminish the asset's value in the company's portfolio.

- **Potential for Preference Creation:** While not an undervalued transaction, granting security may lead to preferential treatment of certain creditors. Such preferences, especially if they unduly favour specific creditors, can be contested and potentially reversed.

This refined explanation encapsulates the critical elements of how transactions at undervalue are addressed in insolvency proceedings. It highlights the need for equitable treatment of all creditors and safeguards against the unfair diminishment of a debtor's asset pool.

4.4 Enhancing the Explanation of Fraudulent Trading in Insolvency Law

Fraudulent trading involves conducting a company's business deliberately intending to defraud creditors. It's not limited to directors; anyone knowingly engaging in such activities can be implicated. Legal proceedings for fraudulent trading can be initiated by either a liquidator or an administrator during insolvency processes.

Legal Consequences and Liability:

(a) **Directors' Liability:** When fraudulent trading is proven in court, directors (or other involved parties) may be ordered to contribute to the company's assets to compensate for the fraud.

(b) **Criminal Offence:** Beyond civil liability, fraudulent trading is also recognised as a criminal act, potentially leading to more severe legal consequences.

Practical Challenges in Prosecution:

(a) **Proving Intent:** Successfully proving fraudulent trading in court is challenging. It requires clear evidence of intent to defraud creditors, which is often difficult to establish conclusively.

(b) **A rarity in Practice:** Due to these challenges, legally established fraudulent trading instances are relatively rare.

This enhanced explanation sheds light on the complexities and legal implications of fraudulent trading in the context of insolvency law. It underscores the serious nature of such conduct and the stringent proof requirements to establish guilt.

4.5 Elaborating on Wrongful Trading in Insolvency Law

Wrongful trading refers to situations where directors continue to operate a company despite knowing or having sufficient reason to know that insolvency is inevitable. The pivotal moment in wrongful trading is when directors' primary duty shifts from shareholders' interests to minimising potential losses for the company's creditors.

Legal Proceedings and Responsibility:

(a) **Initiation of Action:** Actions for wrongful trading can be instituted by a liquidator or an administrator during the insolvency process.

(b) **Potential Court Orders:** Successful litigation can lead to court orders mandating directors to make personal financial contributions to the company's assets. This is determined based on what the court considers appropriate.

Defence Against Wrongful Trading Claims:

(a) **Proactive Steps for Minimising Loss:** Directors can defend themselves against wrongful trading allegations by demonstrating that they took every conceivable step to minimise potential loss to creditors after realising that insolvency was unavoidable.

(b) **Importance of Proactive Measures:** In potential insolvency scenarios, directors are expected to be proactive. This includes seeking and adhering to professional advice rather than adopting a passive approach.

(c) **Threshold for Defence:** The defence's success hinges on showing that the director actively and reasonably worked to reduce the impact of impending insolvency on creditors.

4.6 Analysis of Setting Aside a Floating Charge in Insolvency

Floating charges are typically security interests granted over a company's assets, such as inventory, which are subject to change over time. In insolvency cases, floating charges can be automatically considered void, thus not requiring a court's intervention under specific conditions.

The **critical factors for a floating charge** to be considered automatically void are:

(a) **Timeframe:** The charge was created within 12 months before the onset of insolvency (extended to two years if the beneficiary is a connected person to the company).

(b) **Consideration Aspect:** The charge was granted without consideration (i.e., without the company receiving anything in return).

(c) **Insolvency Status:** Either the company was insolvent when creating the charge, or it became insolvent due to the granting of the charge. This requirement does not apply if the charge is to a connected person.

Implications for Liquidators and Administrators:

(a) **Ease of Process:** The automatic void nature of such floating charges facilitates the process for liquidators or administrators, eliminating the need for legal action to invalidate these charges.

(b) **Recovery of Assets:** Voiding these charges enables a more straightforward recovery of assets, potentially increasing the funds available for distribution among creditors.

(c) **Connected Persons' Charges:** Special attention is given to charges favouring connected persons, indicating heightened scrutiny to prevent preferential treatment or abuse.

This understanding of the automatic voiding of floating charges under insolvency law highlights the legal mechanisms to ensure equitable treatment of creditors and the fair distribution of a company's assets in insolvency situations.

Imagine a company, TechWidgets Ltd., experiencing financial difficulties. To secure additional funding, it grants a floating charge over its inventory to SpeedyLoans, a lending institution, ten months before facing insolvency. TechWidgets Ltd. received no direct financial benefit or consideration in return for this charge.

As TechWidgets Ltd. approaches insolvency, the liquidator examines the company's financial transactions and discovers the floating charge granted to SpeedyLoans. The following points are considered:

Timeframe of the Floating Charge: The charge was created within 12 months of TechWidgets Ltd.'s insolvency.

Lack of Consideration: TechWidgets Ltd. did not receive any financial consideration from SpeedyLoans for this charge, making it gratuitous.

Company's Insolvency Status: When the charge was created, the company was on the brink of insolvency. The liquidator determined that the company was already struggling financially, and the creation of the floating charge did not improve its position.

Given these circumstances, the liquidator deems the floating charge automatically void. TechWidgets Ltd.'s inventory, which was subject to the floating charge, is now available to be liquidated for all creditors, not just SpeedyLoans. This ensures a fairer distribution of the company's remaining assets among its creditors.

In this scenario, SpeedyLoans, despite having a floating charge, is treated like other unsecured creditors, unable to claim preferential treatment over TechWidgets Ltd.'s assets in the insolvency proceedings.

4.7 Explanation of Ring Fencing in Liquidation

In corporate liquidation, "ring-fencing" refers to a legal mechanism that protects a portion of the company's assets for the benefit of unsecured creditors. This protection is particularly relevant when dealing with assets subject to a floating charge.

The concept of ring-fencing ensures that unsecured creditors, who often stand last in line for repayment in a liquidation process, receive a fair share of the company's remaining assets.

Critical Points of Ring Fencing:

(a) **Allocation of Assets:** A particular portion of the assets covered by floating charges is specifically earmarked or 'ring-fenced' to be distributed among unsecured creditors.

(b) Percentage Allocation:

- The first £100,000 of assets subject to floating charges are divided such that 50% of this value is set aside for unsecured creditors.

- For assets above £100,000 subject to floating charges, 20% is ring-fenced for unsecured creditors.

(c) **Maximum Limit:** The total amount in the ring-fenced fund is capped at £600,000. This means that even if the value of assets subject to floating charges is significantly higher, the amount allocated for unsecured creditors will not exceed £600,000.

(d) **Purpose:** The primary goal is to ensure a more equitable distribution of assets in liquidation, particularly to unsecured creditors who otherwise face higher risks of not recovering their debts.

(e) **Impact on Secured Creditors:** While secured creditors with floating charges have a priority claim on certain assets, the ring-fencing mechanism slightly reduces their share in favour of unsecured creditors.

(f) **Legal Basis:** This provision is part of the UK insolvency law, intended to balance the interests of different classes of creditors during the liquidation process.

Suppose XYZ Ltd. is undergoing liquidation and has £500,000 worth of assets subject to floating charges. The calculation for ring-fenced funds would be:

- 50% of the first £100,000 = £50,000

- 20% of the remaining £400,000 = £80,000

So, the total ring-fenced fund for unsecured creditors would be £130,000.

CONCLUSION

As we have explored throughout "Business Law and Practice" the intricacies of the legal framework are both profound and extensive.

In conclusion, let this book be both your guide and your invitation to engage deeply with the law. May it inspire you to continue learning, questioning, and shaping the legal landscape of England and Wales.

REFERENCES

MacIntyre, E. (2014). Business Law. Pearson.

Marson, J. (2019). Business Law Concentrate: Law Revision and Study Guide by James Marson. Oxford University Press.

Kelly, D., Hammer, R., Denoncourt, J., Hendy, J. (2020). Business Law. Routledge.

ABOUT AUTHORS

Anastasia & Andrew Vialichka have authored a revered collection of study guides and quizzes (metexam.co.uk), addressing the full spectrum of topics tested by the Solicitors Qualifying Examination (SQE). Their portfolio encompasses thorough treatments of *Business Law and Practice, Dispute Resolution, Contract, Tort, Legal System of England and Wales, Constitutional and Administrative Law and EU Law, Legal Services, Property Law and Practice, Wills and the Administration of Estates, Solicitors Accounts, Land Law, Trusts, Criminal Law and Practice, Equity, etc*

Authors' works are not only informational but also innovative, incorporating AI-based technology to enhance test preparation. This modern approach tailors learning to individual styles, aiding students to master both the theory and practice required for the SQE.

Printed in Great Britain
by Amazon